The Evolving American Presidency

Series Editor
Michael A. Genovese
Loyola Marymount University
Los Angeles, California
USA

This series is stimulated by the clash between the presidency as invented and the presidency as it has developed. Over time, the presidency has evolved and grown in power, expectations, responsibilities, and authority. Adding to the power of the presidency have been wars, crises, depressions, industrialization. The importance and power of the modern presidency makes understanding it so vital. How presidents resolve challenges and paradoxes of high expectations with limited constitutional resources is the central issue in modern governance and the central theme of this book series.

More information about this series at
http://www.springer.com/series/14437

Michael A. Genovese • David Gray Adler

The War Power in an Age of Terrorism

Debating Presidential Power

Michael A. Genovese
Political Science
Loyola Marymount University
Los Angeles
California
USA

David Gray Adler
President, Alturas Institute
Alturas, Idaho, USA
and
Lecturer, University of Idaho
College of Law, Idaho Falls, Idaho, USA

The Evolving American Presidency
ISBN 978-1-137-59353-5   ISBN 978-1-137-57931-7 (eBook)
DOI 10.1057/978-1-137-57931-7

Library of Congress Control Number: 2016956866

Cover illustration: Pattern adapted from an Indian cotton print produced in the 19th century

Printed on acid-free paper

This Palgrave Macmillan imprint is published by Springer Nature
The registered company is Nature America Inc.
The registered company address is: 1 New York Plaza, New York, NY 10004, U.S.A.

PREFACE AND ACKNOWLEDGMENTS

In wartime, the Constitution needs all the friends it can get. The fog of war clouds our vision, and we often act before we think. Or we act before we have sufficient information. Thus, we often overreact, or rush to judgment.

Such was the case in the aftermath of 9/11. In our effort to fight terrorism, we overstepped, putting key constitutional guarantees of rights in jeopardy. We also embraced a nuclear, imperial presidency, and policies that backfired on us, and unleashed a torrent of wicked problems from which we still suffer.

To be fair, the people in the White House did not know if the initial attack on 9/11 was the beginning of a more massive attack; they operated in a world of uncertainty and confusion; and believed another major assault on the United States might be imminent. Put yourself in their shoes. Would you have acted in a measured, thoughtful way, fully conscious of protecting rights of citizens, or would you have been primarily concerned with preventing another attack and saving the lives of citizens?

Much ink has been spilled blaming, first, President Bush, and later President Obama for their excessive zeal in fighting the threats of terrorism. We need not engage that argument, and assign blame. The concern here is to look afresh at the war powers in the United States as we emerge out of our post-9/11 fog.

In an age of terrorism, does, should, can, our original constitutional structure for declaring war still guide us? Is our eighteenth-century Constitution hopelessly out of date for a twenty-first-century superpower? So let us revisit the founders of our system to glean insights into their goals, see how that system operates in our world, and ask, "Should we still be guided by their model?"

There is no more important decision governments make than to go to war. Asking citizens to risk their lives, committing the resources of the nation, jeopardizing the very existence of the nation, is a monumental decision fraught with consequences of the highest magnitude.

How does the United States enter into war? Who decides? On what basis? Within what confines?

This is a book about how we go to war. We present the ideal and constitutional (the U.S. Congress authorizes war, either by a formal declaration or by joint resolution), and the real and political (most often, the president merely acts, taking the nation into war).

We will also look at the how the post–September 11, 2001, war against terrorism has placed new strains on the war powers, and how the United States has responded to this new threat.

In the end, we will argue that at least since the end of World War II, the war power has been hijacked by an Imperial Presidency, and often ceded to the executive by a feckless Congress. Unfortunately, an untutored American public has mistakenly attributed to the president the authority to initiate war, an error that has been promoted by an equally untutored press. For the sake of constitutionalism, the rule of law, the separation of powers, and our system of checks and balances, we had better turn this around and "get it right," or else the vitality and integrity of our constitutional republic are in jeopardy.

The format of this book is to present an argument over the role of constitutionalism and presidential power in an age of terrorism. One author takes the position that the original war declaring power of Congress needs to be updated to better suit a twenty-first-century super-power. The other author believes that we can and should hold true to the vision of the Framers, and continue to invest in the power to authorize war in the hands of the Congress. We present this friendly argument as a vehicle for readers to make more thoughtful and informed decisions on who shall take the nation into war.

As you will see, the authors differ regarding just what should be done—if anything—about the war powers in the United States. One author (Genovese) argues that a twenty-first-century superpower needs a more streamlined—modern—system of going to war. The other author (Adler) is a staunch defender of the Framers' model and argues that its values are as compelling today as they were at the time of the framing of the Constitution. If there is friendly disagreement, there is also a place where the two authors agree. And it is in that area of agreement—retroactive justification—that both authors find common ground in a complex world.

One more thing we both agree on is that we Americans have yet to take a cold, hard look at constitutionalism in an age of terrorism. We hope this book takes us one step closer to doing just that.

Michael A. Genovese thanks the students who helped manage him and the manuscript preparation: John Pickhaver, Dani Jordan, and Jake Weitz, who were always helpful, usually cheerful, and chronically hardworking. David Gray Adler thanks his many students and colleagues over the years at Idaho State University and the University of Idaho College of Law, for listening to his views on the war power; the Idaho Humanities Council for generous support of this project; the Board of Directors of the Alturas Institute for their enthusiasm, vision, encouragement, and support: Steve Carr, Doug Oppenheimer, Clay Morgan, Barbara Morgan, Caroline Heldman, Jeff Neiswanger, Mark Young, and Tim Hopkins; Kelli Jenkins for her superb administrative skills, and Penni Englert, for her wonderful clerical assistance.

CONTENTS

CHAPTER 1

War and American Democracy

THE KING (in disguise): Methinks I could not die anywhere so contented as in the King's company, his cause being just...

WILLIAMS (a solider): But if the cause be not good, the King himself hath a heavy reckoning to make when all those legs and arms and heads, chopped off in a battle, shall join together at the latter day and cry all, "We died at such a place," some swearing, some crying for a surgeon, some upon their wives left poor behind them...

–Shakespeare's King Henry V: in the English camp, the night before the battle of Agincourt

In questions of power, then, let no more be said of confidence in man, but bind him down from mischief by the chains of the constitution.

–Thomas Jefferson, Kentucky Resolution of 1798

They that can give up essential liberty to obtain a little temporary safety deserve neither liberty nor safety.

–Benjamin Franklin

Abstract The beginning of the book sets the background for the discussion and debate that follows. The book opens with the new challenges posed by a post-9/11 world in which terrorism is the new enemy. We look at an old problem—the war power—in light of new circumstances—terrorism. To draw insights into the contemporary controversy, we look back at the Framers of the American system and what they sought to do at the

© The Author(s) 2017
M.A. Genovese, D.G. Adler, *The War Power in an Age of Terrorism*, The Evolving American Presidency,
DOI 10.1057/978-1-137-57931-7_1

Constitutional Convention to "tame the dogs of war." This led to the Framers giving to Congress, not the president, the sole authority to authorize or declare war. We explore the debates and decisions made by the Framers, discuss the ratification debate, and how the assertion of the war power has changed over time.

Keywords War · War power · Executive authority · President · Presidency · Power · Plenary powers · Unilateral powers · Shared powers · Constitution · Congress

INTRODUCTION

The U.S. constitutional allocation of war powers, and the separation-of-powers and checks and balances so deeply associated with it, are going through a period of profound turmoil and change. The turmoil is a result of the aftermath of September 11, 2001, terrorist attack against the United States and the resulting war against international terrorism that it spawned. The change has been brought on by the bold, assertive, and largely unchallenged assertion of independent, plenary power claimed first by the Bush administration as it prosecuted the war against terrorism, and later by the Obama administration. And while the rhetoric of the Obama administration toned down the broad claims of independent presidential authority, in practice they exercised power independent of Congress—a "Bush Lite" model.[1]

These changes threatened the very fabric of the rule of law and separation of powers embedded in the U.S. States Constitution. If allowed to go unchallenged, this presidential claim of authority would bring us full circle from the 1770s and a revolution against the perceived arbitrary and personal power of the King, to the outright rejection of the British model in the new Constitution, and embrace of the republican government grounded in the separation of powers, to an Imperial presidency, back full circle to a form of elected monarchical power.

It is not unfounded alarmism that draws one to this conclusion but the hard-nosed reality of power as practiced in the post-9/11 age. The Bush administration claimed expansive and nearly exclusive control over foreign

[1] Chris Edelson, *The Grand Illusion* (Minneapolis: University of Minnesota Press, 2016).

policy and war but also practiced what it preached. The Obama administration is merely less of the same.

This book takes a hard look at the war powers in America, especially in light of the changes that resulted from the war against terrorism. We will look at the war powers in eighteenth-century Britain, the rejection of that model by the Framers of the U.S. Constitution, their new model of the war powers, how that model evolved over time, the rise of American power and the Imperial presidency in the post–World War II era, and the development of the extra-constitutional presidency of George W. Bush. In the end, we will make recommendations for how to reassert the rule of law, constitutionalism, and accountability into the war powers.

THE PREDICATE

On the morning of September 11, 2001, terrorists hijacked four commercial airplanes. Two were flown into the World Trade Center in New York City, one into the Pentagon in Washington, D.C., and one was downed by brave passengers in the fields of Pennsylvania before it could be flown into its intended target.

It is the image of the two planes crashing into the towers of the World Trade Center that is indelibly etched in the minds of most Americans.

The United States has been attacked! Were we at war? Against whom? How should we respond?

Indeed, a new kind of state of war did exist, and the president responded. It is emblematic of the decline of the war powers and the constitutional moorings of modern American politics that the public, and Congress, virtually everyone looked to one person to respond: the president.

In the modern age, the president has trumped Congress, the Constitution, and the rule of law and emerged as the nation's first responder, crisis-manager-in-chief, war lord, and Imperial leader.

As the president acts, the Congress sheepishly looks on, its power sapped by the presidential initiative and congressional acquiescence. And as the president acts, the Constitution is caught beneath the drumbeat of war.

On September 14, 2001, the United States Senate and House of Representatives responding to a demand by President George W. Bush, and with the support of the American public, hastily and overwhelmingly granted the president authority to use "all necessary and appropriate force," and take military action "in order to prevent any further acts of international terrorism."

Was this a formal declaration of war our Constitution seems to require? No. Was it a broad congressional authorization for presidential war making? Yes. In fact, it reads like a "blank check" for authorizing the president to do "whatever it takes" to fight this war against terrorism.

We can blame President Bush for much that went wrong in the war against terrorism: poor planning the lead up to the Iraq War, failure to adequately equip the troops, incompetent war execution, extraordinary rendition, the use of torture, trampling on the Constitutional rights of U.S. citizens, illegal domestic spying, dishonesty in making the case for war against Iraq, and callous disregard in the care of wounded veterans who returned from war.

But if the predicate was September 11, the enabler was Congress. It handed the president breathtakingly broad authorization with little supervision or accountability. Yes, blame President Bush for incompetence and mismanagement; but blame also the Congress for failing to adequately fulfill its constitutional duties, and the people, too, for gravitating to a knight in shining armor to save them.

Swept up in a whirlwind of emotion as the dogs of war were unleashed, Congress handed to the president the war power on a silver platter. To the public, perhaps, this ascribed some legitimacy to the war for it sensed congressional support even if it was unaware of the constitutional principles that govern the decision to go to war on behalf of the American people. But a rubber stamp Congress is no real Congress, and merely handing power over to the executive is not a fulfillment, but an abandonment of congressional constitutional responsibility.

It was not the first such congressional failure.

Thirty-seven years earlier, an eerily tight parallel to the September 14 congressional vote occurred when Congress, by virtually the same vote as took place authorizing the Iraq War, nearly unanimously approved the Gulf of Tonkin Resolution (1964) giving President Lyndon Johnson a blank check in Vietnam. Ironically, Johnson, like Bush, was later accused of misleading Congress in the run up to the war.

Both congressional votes proved to be monumental errors, as first the war in Vietnam, and later the war in Iraq went horribly wrong. The war in Vietnam led to the failed congressional effort to reclaim some of the war powers it seemed so willing to hand over to the president. But the War Powers Resolution of 1973 did not change the equation. Indeed, the twisted measure mistakenly conferred upon the president authority to wage war for 60 days without congressional authorization, a grant of power that violates the fundamental principle of the War Clause.

How did we repeat the errors of our past? Why did we not learn the lesson of Vietnam and its aftermath?

In light of the repeated mistakes of the past as well as our current constitutional troubles, it makes sense to reexamine the war powers and the rule of law in an age of terrorism.

President Bush had claimed that his war against terrorism was a "different" type of war—it is being fought, not against the traditional enemy—the nation-state—but against a shadowy enemy organization of terrorist cells scattered across the globe. Can the war against terrorism be fought within our constitutional framework of separation of powers, checks, and balances, and the rule of law? Or—for the nation's safety and security—must we abandon the Constitution in favor of a more centralized, executive-driven war-fighting capability? Is our Constitution, written for an eighteenth-century nation, sufficient for a twenty-first-century superpower?

THE PROBLEM

The Imperial Presidency of George W. Bush reanimated the debate about the scope and contour of the war power. Of course its roots date, at least, to the post-World War II period. Earlier presidents had aggrandized power, sometimes in clearly unconstitutional ways, but the powerful chief executives of the past took great pains to ground their power grabs in the patina of constitutionalism, always acknowledging that the Constitution was king. Lincoln during the Civil War, Wilson in World War I, and FDR in World War II acknowledged that while their actions may have exceeded normal practice, they were nonetheless bound to respect constitutional limits and the rule of law.

It was not until after World War II with the onset of the Cold War that presidents began to claim plenary, inherent, independent power, either grounded (mistakenly) in the Constitution or in authority stemming from the office itself. During the Korean War in the 1950s, President Harry Truman claimed independent authority (as commander in chief) to commit U.S. troops to combat. This, of course, violated both the spirit and letter of the Constitution, but in the atmosphere of Cold War hysteria, few had the courage to challenge the president. And yet, it is in just such times that the Constitution needs friends, and all the defenders it can muster.

From that point on, presidents made grander and grander claims of unilateral, independent power, which led to the emergence of what in the 1970s historian, Arthur M. Schlesinger, Jr. described as an *Imperial Presidency.*

TAMING THE AMERICAN PRINCE

Constitutionalism and the rule of law emerged in the United States out of the ashes of hereditary monarchies and the arbitrary powers of the king. In England, especially during the 1600s, the struggle for power between the king and nascent Parliament produced a slow, often violent conflict, directed toward the effort by parliamentarians to tame the powers of the king, and limit the authority of the crown. From the Magna Carta in 1215, to the British Civil War of the 1640s, to the beheading of Charles I in 1649, to the Glorious Revolution of 1688, and beyond, Parliaments and Kings battled for control of power.[2] Over time, kings were compelled to reluctantly give up powers to the Parliament as the process of harnessing executive power brought the rule of kings under the control of legislative authority and the rule of law.

When the Americas were colonized, the Age of the Divine Rights of Kings was giving way to more limited and representative forms of power. During the Divine Right of Kings, a monarch could *Rule or Command.* After all, he claimed his authority based on the will of God. To challenge the king was to challenge God. For a king, this was very firm ground on which to stand. But it left the people with little to cling to except the "good will" of the king. But as the church and the barons challenged the King's power, a long, slow, often violent transformation took place. The Divine Right of Kings was slowly replaced by the Divine Right of the People (Democracy through their representatives).[3] Both the American and the French Revolutions directly challenged the central authority of the king, and sought to create a more representative or democratic system.

In this new political configuration, authority and legitimacy that once came from God now came from something called "the People." This new secular base or authority replaced command; influence and persuasion

---

[2] See: Geoffrey Robertson, *The Tyrannicide Brief* (London: Vintage Books, 2006).

[3] Edmund S. Morgan, *Inventing the People* (New York: Norton, 1988).

replaced orders. Government officials had to lead, not command. Eventually, rule of the people through elected representatives made the government the servant of the people through their laws. "In America," Tom Paine pointed out, "the law is king."[4]

The American Revolution took place in the middle of this transformation. As liberal democracy emerged "the leader" (aka, the king) was seen as the problem to be solved, not as the solution to the people's problem. To the colonists, the king became the focal point, the magnet of all complaints and criticisms. At the time of the colonists' break with Great Britain, anti-monarchical sentiment was strong. Jefferson's *Declaration of Independence* was, in addition to being an eloquent expression of democratic and revolutionary faith, a laundry list of charges leveled against the tyrannical king. And propagandist supreme, Tom Paine, stigmatized England's King George III as "The Royal Brute of Britain."

Jefferson's brilliant prose conjures up a panoply of revolutionary fervor inspiring a rush of democratic sentiment. The appeal to reason, the bold language and even bolder message, the call to arms, the proclamation of universal rights, all leave the reader with democratic fervor. From the preamble to the last ringing chorus, the men of the founding era were truly men for the ages. The preamble of the Declaration of Independence runs thus:

> When, in the course of human events, it becomes necessary for one people to dissolve the political bands which have connected them with another, and to assume, among the powers of earth, the separate and equal station to which the laws of nature and of nature's God entitle then, a decent respect to the opinions of mankind requires that they should declare the causes which impel them to separate.

That was only the beginning. Yes, the Declaration asserted on behalf of the colonists, we are breaking our bond with the past, and this is why we do so:

> We hold these truths to be self-evident, that all men are created equal, that they are endowed by their Creator with certain unalienable Rights, that among these are Life, Liberty and the pursuit of Happiness.

---

[4] *Thomas Paine's Common Sense: The Call to Independence*, ed. Thomas Wendel (New York: Barron's, 1975, 1998).

> That to secure these rights, Governments are instituted among Men, deriving their just powers from the consent of the governed.
> That whenever any Form of Government becomes destructive of these ends, it is the Right of the People to alter or to abolish it, and to institute new Government, laying its foundation on such principles and organizing its powers in such form, as to them shall seem most likely to effect their Safety and Happiness. Prudence, indeed, will dictate that Governments long established should not be changed for light and transient causes; and accordingly all experience hath shewn, that mankind are more disposed to suffer, while evils are sufferable, than to right themselves by abolishing the forms to which they are accustomed. But when a long train of abuses and usurpations, pursuing invariably the same Object evinces a design to reduce them under absolute Despotism, it is their right, it is their duty, to throw off such Government, and to provide new Guards for their future security.

The language is crisp, clear, strong, to the point, and dripping with powerful prose and imagery. These inspiring words declare guiding principles as well as independence. And to drive their point home, the remainder of the *Declaration of Independence* is a long list of crimes and grievances directed against the British Crown. The bill of particulars leveled against King George III included:

> repeating injuries and usurpations
> He has refused his assent to laws . . .
> He has obstructed the administration of justice . . .
> He has made judged dependent of his will alone . . .
> He has erected a multitude of new offices and sent hither swarms of officers to harass our people and eat out their substance . . .
> He has affected to render the military independent of, and superior to, the civil power . . .
> He has combined with others to subject us to jurisdiction foreign to our constitution and unacknowledged by our laws . . .
> For taking away our charters, abolishing our most valuable laws, and altering, fundamentally, the forms of our government.

Sadly, much of this sounds tragically familiar in our age. And while no one would make the case that we have literally replaced a king of England with a king of America, the ubiquitous presence of the American presidency and the precipitous growth of presidential power in the modern era leaves one to draw frightening parallels.

Anti-executive feelings were so strong among the American rebels that when the post-revolutionary leadership assembled to form a government, their *Articles of Confederation* contained—amazingly—no executive! Yet, so weak and ineffective were the Articles that Noah Webster said they were "but a name, and our confederation a cobweb."[5] Over time, the absence of an executive proved unworkable, and slowly and grudgingly the need for an executive became accepted. At the Constitutional Convention, James Wilson was the first to raise the possibility of a single executive officer for the new government, and his comment was met, according to James Madison' s notes, with "a considerable pause"—so anti-executive were the delegates that even the thought of a new kingly officer led to harsh looks and stunned silence. But Edmund Randolph of Virginia broke the silence reminding the delegates that there would be "no semblance of a monarch" in the new government.

James Madison's view on the importance of controlling the power to declare war and limiting executive power, stemmed from his belief that war was the greatest threat to republican government. "Of all the enemies of public liberties war is, perhaps, the most to be dreaded, because it comprises and develops the germ of every other. War is the parent of armies; from these proceed debts and taxes; and armies and debts, and taxes are the known instruments for bringing the many under the domination of the few." Military conflict also expanded executive power to dangerous extremes. "No nation could preserve its freedom in the midst of continual warfare." And he would later note that, "The constitution supposes, what the History of all Governments demonstrates, that the Executive is the branch ... most interested in war, and prone to it."[6]

Alexander Hamilton addressed the Convention on June 18, 1787 and delivered a speech praising the British system as "the best in the world." "The British monarchy is," he told delegates, "the only good model of

---

[5] See: Noah Webster, *Sketches of American Policy*, ed. Harry R. Warfel (New York: Scholar's Facsimiles & Reprints 1937).

[6] "Political Observations," April 20, 1795, in *The Papers of James Madison* (PJM), 17 vols, eds. William T. Hutchinson and William M.E. Rachel (Chicago: Chicago University Press; Charlottesville: University of Virginia Press, 1962–1991), 15: 511–534; JM to Thomas Jefferson, April 2, 1797. *JMW*, 586; See also: Jeff Broadwater, "James Madison on the Vices of the American Political System Today," *Extensions*, June 2014, pp. 5–9.

executive power available." But Hamilton was waxing philosophical and never proposed powers for an American presidency that even remotely resembled those possessed by the English king. Indeed, he argued in Philadelphia for a constrained executive that echoed the views of Madison and Wilson. The Framers' fear of an embryonic monarchy meant that the executive would possess only limited powers.

As the Framers met in Philadelphia, most of those present recognized the need for an independent executive with *some* power. But how to both empower and tame this new prince? No useful model existed anywhere in the known world. They would have to invent one.

INVENTING A PRESIDENCY

The American Revolution against Great Britain was a revolt against both parliamentary and executive authority. Historian Bernard Bailyn said the rebellion against Britain made resistance to central authority a divine doctrine.[7] The colonists were for the most part independent, egalitarian, and individualistic. Their symbols and rallying cries were antiauthority in nature and when it became necessary to establish a new government, it was difficult to reestablish the respect for authority so necessary for an effective government.

Thus, reconstructing executive authority, out of the ashes of revolution, was a slow process. By 1787, when the Framers met in Philadelphia to revise the Articles of Confederation, there was an agreement that a limited executive was necessary to promote good government, but what kind of executive? One person or several? How should he be selected? For how long a term? With what power? [8]

No decision at the Convention was more difficult to reach than the scope and nature of the executive. They went through proposals, counterproposals, decisions, reconsiderations, postponements, and reversals until finally a presidency was invented.[9] The confusion reflected what political scientist

---

[7] See: Bernard Bailyn, *The Ideological Origins of the American Revolution* (Cambridge, MA: Harvard University Press, 1967), Chapter 4 (Bailyn 1967).

[8] See: Charles C. Thatch Jr., *The Creation of the Presidency, 1775–1789: A Study in Constitutional History* (Baltimore, MD: Johns Hopkins University Press, 1923).

[9] Thomas E. Cronin ed., *Inventing the American Presidency* (Lawrence: University Press of Kansas, 1989). (Cronin 1989).

Harvey C. Mansfield, Jr. referred to as the Framers' "ambivalence of executive power."[10] Initially, most delegates were considered "congressionalists," hoping to create a government with a strong Congress and a plural executive with limited power. Delegate George Mason proposed the creation of a three-person executive, one chosen from each region of the new nation. Delegate Roger Sherman described this executive, according to the notes from the Constitutional Convention, as "no more than an institution for carrying the will of the legislature into effect."[11] A single executive still conjured images of Imperial power of the king. Virginia Governor Edmund Randolph warned the delegates that it was "the fetus of monarchy."[12] But there were also advocates for a stronger executive.

James Madison, referred to as the father of the Constitution, expressed in the run up to the Convention his own uncertainty about a presidency. He wrote to George Washington on April 16, 1787: "I have scarcely ventured as yet to form my own opinion either of the manner in which [the executive] ought to be constituted or of the authorities with which it ought to be clothed."[13] Probably the most influential Framer on the invention of the presidency was James Wilson of Pennsylvania. Initially, Wilson sought the direct popular election of the president, but eventually lost that battle and instead helped develop what became the Electoral College. He also greatly influenced the choice of a single over a plural executive.

In the end, the Framers attempted to strike a balance in executive power. Making the presidency too strong would jeopardize liberty; making the office too weak would jeopardize good government. But just how to achieve balance remained a thorny issue. Unlike the Congress and the Judiciary, for which there was ample precedent to guide them, the

---

[10] See: Harvey C. Mansfield, Jr., *Taming the Prince: The Ambivalence of Modern Executive Power* (New York: Free Press, 1989), Chapter 1.

[11] "The Debates in the Federal Convention of 1787 Reported by James Madison: June 1," the Avalon Project at Yale Law School, available at http://avalon.law.yale.edu/18th_century/debates_601.asp. Accessed May 14, 2006.

[12] Quoted in Jack N. Rabove, *Original Meanings* (New York: Knopf, 1996), p. 257.

[13] James Madison, letter to Weedon Butler, May 5, 1788, as quoted in S. Sidney Ulmer, "The Role of Pierce Butler in the Constitutional Convention," *Review of Politics* 22 (July 1960), pp. 361–374.

presidency was truly new, invented in Philadelphia, and different from any executive office that preceded it. The president would not be a king, he would not be sovereign. He would swear to protect and defend the higher authority: the Constitution, and the law.

The Framers faced several key questions. First, how many? Should there be a single (unitary) or plural executive? Initial sympathy for a plural executive gave way to a single executive, primarily because that was the best was to assign responsibility (and blame) in the execution of policy. The second question was how to choose the executive. Some proposed popular election, which was rejected because the Framers feared the president might become tribune of the people. Others promoted selection by Congress. This was rejected on the grounds that it might make the president the servant of Congress, and undermine the separation of powers. Finally, the Framers invented an Electoral College as the best of several unappealing alternatives.

Next, how long should he serve? Should the president serve for life? A fixed term? Two years, four years, six years? If for a fixed term, should he be eligible for re-election? After much hemming and hawing they decided on a four-year term with re-eligibility as an option. But the president could be removed—impeached—for various offenses against the state.

The most difficult question that the Framers faced with respect to the creation of the presidency was the scope of constitutional authority to vest in the office. Their fear of executive power, derived from their own experience under King George III and their reading of history, affirmed Madison's advice that the powers of the executive should be "confined and defined." The sketch of powers granted to the president in Article II of the Constitution—lean and meager compared to those granted to Congress—reflected their understanding that the president's role consisted largely of faithfully executing the laws and making appointments to office. To a degree, their task was eased by the expectation, and likelihood, that George Washington would be America's first president. So confident were they (and the public as well) of Washington's skills, integrity, and republican sentiments that they possessed a high degree of confidence that Washington would perform his duties and responsibilities in an exemplary manner, worthy of emulation by his successors.

Of course, Washington would not always be the president. Thus, while the Framers trusted Washington, could they trust his successors? Leaving the presidency unfinished opened the door for future problems in the executive. Benjamin Franklin pointed this out when he noted, at the Constitutional Convention on June 4, 1787, "[T]he first man put at the helm will be a good one. Nobody knows what sort may come afterwards."[14]

If there were doubts or disagreements about the exercise of executive power, the unanimity of the delegates in vesting in Congress the sole and exclusive authority to authorize or declare war made it clear beyond all doubt that the president possessed no monarchical authority to commence war.

Did the Framers envision any added reservoir of power for the executive in times of war or national emergency? If they had so intended, they had two options to assign to the presidency, extra power in times of crisis—the Lockean Prerogative—or the Roman temporary crisis authority.

John Locke, in his *Second Treatise of Government*, argued that the executive has the "prerogative" authority to make decisions in emergencies, for the good of the state. In relations between states, the executive might at times do "many things...which the laws do not prescribe." There were times also when the executive could go against the law. Locke defined prerogative as

> this power to act according to discretion for the public good, without the prescription of the law and sometimes against it...Whilst employed for the benefit of the community and suitably to the trust and ends of government...Is [un]questioned. For the people are very seldom or never scrupulous or nice in the point of questioning of prerogative whilst it is in any tolerable degree employed for the use it was meant—that is the good of the people and not manifestly against it...[15]

The Framers were quite familiar with Locke's prerogative, and chose not to include this in the president's power arsenal.

---

[14] "The Debates in the Federal Convention of 1787 Reported by James Madison: June 4," the Avalon Project at Yale Law School, available at http://avalon.law.yale.edu/18th_century/debates_604.asp. Accessed May 14, 2006.

[15] See Locke's *Second Treatise*, Chs XIV, as well as XII, and XIII. See also Thomas S. Langston and Michael E. Lind, "John Locke and the Limits of Presidential Prerogative," *Polity* XXIV, No. 1 (Fall 1991), pp. 49–68. Benjamin A. Kleinerman, "Can the Princes Really Be Tamed? Executive Prerogative, Popular Apathy, and the Constitutional Frame in Locke's Second Treatise," *American Political Science Review* 101, No. 2 (May 2007), pp. 209–222.

Second, in Republican Rome, the office of *dictator* (Latin for "one who dictates or orders") or *Magister Popului* (master of the people) or the *Praetor Maximus* (supreme magistrate) or *Magister Peditum* (magistrate of the infinity) might from time to time be called upon to perform extraordinary or crisis related tasks.

The Roman Senate would, in extraordinary and demanding times, pass a *senatus consultation*, authorizing the *consuls* (leaders) to nominate a temporary dictator. Ordinarily, a dictator was appointed for a six-month period, and in that time, the dictator had extra constitutional powers. Once the crisis that precipitated the appointment of a dictator had passed, all powers reverted back to the Senate.

The Framers were well aware of this as well and could have included such a provision in the Constitution. They chose not to.

How did they choose to assign the war power—the constitutional authority to authorize or declare war? Soured by their experience with the British king, they wanted to insure that the decision to go to war was *not* in the hands of one man. The Framers feared the arbitrary power of the king, feared the light, frivolous, and misguided reasons one man might use to take the nation into war, and feared the consequences of unchecked executive power.

Delegate Charles Pinckney of South Carolina warned that to give the executive power over "peace and war . . . would render the executive a monarchy of the worst kind, to wit an elective one." Pinckney's colleague from South Carolina, John Rutledge agreed, arguing that while he "was for vesting the executive power in a single person," he "was not for giving him the power of war and peace." James Wilson of Pennsylvania sought to reassure the Convention that "the prerogative of the British Monarchy," is not "a proper guide in defining the executive powers. Some of the prerogatives were of a legislative nature. Among others, that of war and peace." James Madison followed Wilson, assuring the Convention that the "executive power . . . do not include the rights of war and peace."

On August 6, the Committee on Detail, presented draft language that included a provision allowing "The legislature . . . to make war." But could a Congress "make war"? Several delegates were skeptical. Pinckney argued that the legislature's "proceedings were too slow" and that wartime decisions might not be amenable to such delays. Pierce Butler, also of South Carolina surprised the Convention by suggesting he "was for vesting the power in the President, who will have all the requisite qualities."

Butler moved that the Convention accept this proposition, which was met with scorn. Elbridge Gerry of Massachusetts said he "never expected to hear in a republic the motion to empower the Executive alone to declare war." Butler's motion failed even to get a second from the floor of the Convention. Madison and Gerry proposed that the Convention substitute "declare" for "make," thereby "leaving to the Executive the power to repel sudden attacks." This was accepted by the Convention.[16]

This brief excerpt from James Madison's notes on the Constitutional Convention dated August 17 tells the story:

Mr. Pinckney opposed vesting [the power to make war] in the Legislature. Its proceedings were too slow. It would meet but once a year. The House of Representatives would be too numerous for such deliberations. The Senate would be the best depositary, being more acquainted with foreign affairs...If the States are equally represented in Senate, so as to give no advantage to large States, the power will notwithstanding be safe, as the small have their all at stake in such cases as well as the large States. It would be singular for one authority to make war, and another peace.

Mr. Butler. The objections against the Legislature lie in great degree against the Senate. He was for vesting the power in the president, who will have all the requisite qualities, and will not make war but when the Nation will support it.

Mr. Madison and Mr. Gerry moved to insert "declare," striking out "make" war; leaving to the Executive the power to repel sudden attacks.

Mr. Sherman thought it stood very well. The Executive should be able to repel and not to commence war. "Make" [is] better than "declare" the latter narrowing the power too much.

Mr. Gerry never expected to hear in a republic a motion to empower the Executive alone to declare war.

Mr. Ellworth. There is a material difference between the cases of making war and making peace. It should be more easy to get out of war than into it. War also is a simple and overt declaration. Peace [is] attended with intricate and secret negotiations.

Mr. Mason was against giving the power of war to the Executive, because [the executive is] not safely to be trusted with it; or to the Senate, because [the Senate is] not so constructed as to be entitled to it. He was for clogging rather than facilitating war; but for facilitating peace. He preferred "declare" to "make."

[16] The Records of the Federal Convention of 1787, Max Ferrard, ed. 1937.

On the motion to insert declare in place of make, it was agreed to [7 yes; 2 no; 1 absent].

... On the remark by Mr. King that "make" war might be understood to "conduct" it, which was an Executive function, Mr. Ellsworth gave up his objection and the vote of Connecticut was changed to ay [8 yes; 1 no; 1 absent].

Mr. Butler moved to give the Legislature power of peace, as they were to have that of war.

Mr. Gerry seconds him. Eight Senators may possibly exercise the power if vested in that body, and fourteen if all should be present; and may consequently give up part of the United States. The Senate are more liable to be corrupted by an Enemy than the whole Legislature

On the motion for adding "and peace" after "war" [0 yes; 10 no].[17]

If the executive did not process the powers of war and peace, who did? *The Congress.*

Article I, section 8 of the United States Constitution, gives the Congress the power "To declare war, grant letters of Marque and Reprisal ... " and other powers. Article II, section 2 says "The President shall be Commander in Chief of the Army and Navy of the United States, and of the Militia of the several states, when called into the actual service of the United States ... "; *when called ... into service.* And who does the calling? *The Congress.*

Congress declares war; the president prosecutes the war. But the president does not do so alone. The Congress maintains a host of other war-related powers, among them: all legislative power, power of the purse, power to maintain and raise as well as regulate the armed forces.[18] Congress was to declare war, but the president was commander in chief. Alexander Hamilton explained in *Federalist No. 69*:

The President is to be commander-in-chief of the army and navy of the United States. In this respect his authority would be nominally the same with that of the king of Great Britain, but in substance much inferior to it. It would amount to nothing more than the supreme command and direction of the military and naval forces, as first General and admiral of the

[17] See: *The Avalon Project*, Yale Law School.

[18] See: Louis Fisher, *Presidential War Power*, 2nd edition (Lawrence: University of Kansas Press, 2004).

Confederacy; while that of the British king extends to the DECLARING of war and to RAISING and REGULATING of fleets and armies, all which, by the Constitution under consideration, would appertain to the legislature.

This dual capacity for war was embedded into the Constitution—the only way the government could legitimately act was with the cooperation of the executive and legislative branches.

As with so many other elements of the new government, the Framers divided and shared the responsibility for war between the president and Congress. The Congress declares or otherwise authorizes war; the president, in his capacity as commander in chief, conducts the war, although he is subject to instructions and directions from Congress throughout the period of hostilities. Congress has declared war on a dozen occasions, and authorized hostilities dozens of others. Early in American history, Congress declared war in the War of 1812, the Mexican War, the Spanish-American War and World War I. In World War II, Congress declared war on six occasions alone. In the many other military conflicts or wars, Congress has either granted the president a legislative authorization (e.g. the first Gulf War), or the president has asserted unilateral authority, as in the Korean War.

The legality and legitimacy of some of the non-declared wars were challenged in the courts. In 1800, in *Bas v. Tingy*, the Supreme Court held that Congress *could* authorize military hostilities without declaring war, thereby giving Congress more options and flexibility. The key was that Congress, as the constitutional repository of the war power, was required to authorize hostilities. The president, it was pointed out, had no authority to initiate war.

The Framers invented a presidency that had some strength, but limited independent power. They put the president in a position to *lead*, but rarely command. The chief mechanisms they established to control as well as to empower the executive were: (1) *Limited Government*, a reaction against the arbitrary, expansive powers of the king or state, and a protection of personal liberty; (2) *Rule of Law*, so that only on the basis of legal or constitutional grounds could the government act; (3) *Separation of Powers*, so that each of the three branches of the government would have a defined sphere of power, and (4) *Checks and Balances*, so that each branch could limit or control the power of the other branches of government.

The Framers of the U.S. Constitution created—by design—what might be called an "antileadership" system. While this may at first sound strange, upon reflection, it should be clear that their primary goal—rather than to provide for any especially efficient system—was to create a government that would not jeopardize liberty. Freedom was their goal, and governmental power their nemesis. Thus the men who toiled on that hot summer of 1787 in Philadelphia created an executive institution, a presidency that had *limited powers*, under the rule of law, in a separation-of-powers system.[19]

DEFENDING THE CONSTITUTION

For James Madison, a government with unchecked power was a dangerous government. A keen student of history, Madison believed that human nature drove men—at this time, only men were allowed to enter the public arena—to pursue self-interest, and therefore a system of government designed to have ambition checked by ambition set within rather strict limits was the only hope to establish a stable government that did not endanger liberty. Realizing that "enlightened statesmen" would not always be at the helm, Madison embraced a check-and-balance system of separate but overlapping and shared powers. Madison's concern to have a government with controlled and limited powers is seen throughout his writings, but nowhere is it more vivid than when he wrote in *Federalist No. 51*, "You must first enable the government to control the governed; and in the next place, oblige it to control itself."[20]

Alexander Hamilton emerged as the defender of executive power in the Federalist Papers as a means of promoting efficient, energetic administration and enforcement of the laws. An advocate of strong central government, Hamilton promoted, especially in the *Federalist Papers*, a version of executive power different from Madison's dispersed and separate powers. Like Madison, who believed that the new government's

---

[19] David Gray Adler, "The Constitution and Presidential Warmaking," in *The Constitution and the Conduct of American Foreign Policy*, eds. Adler and George (Lawrence: University of Kansas Press, 1996), pp. 183–226. (Adler and George 1996).

[20] Alexander Hamilton, "*Federalist No. 45*," in *The Federalist with the Letters of "Brutus,"* ed. Terrence Ball (Cambridge: Cambridge University Press, 2003), 252.

powers should be "few and defined,"[21] Hamilton wanted to infuse the executive with "energy" within the confines of constitutional authority allocated to the president. As Hamilton wrote in *Federalist No. 70*, good government requires "energy," and he scornfully rejected the weak executive: "A feeble executive implies a feeble execution of the government. A feeble execution is but another phrase for bad execution; and a government ill executed, whatever it may be in theory, must be, in practice, a bad government."[22]

Like the rest of his fellow delegates at the Convention, Hamilton advocated congressional authority over the power of war and peace. In *Federalist No. 69*, he wrote that the president's powers as commander in chief "would amount to nothing more than the supreme command and direction of the military and naval forces . . . while that of the British kings extends to declaring of war and to the raising and regulating of the fleets and armies, all which, by the Constitution under consideration would appertain to the legislature." Thus, make him "first General and Admiral" only "in the direction of war when authorized or begun."

Madison reaffirmed Hamilton's distinction in 1793 when he wrote, "those who are to conduct a war cannot in the nature of things, be proper or safe judges whether a war ought to be commenced, continued, or concluded. They are barred from the latter functions by a great principle in free government, analogous to that which separates the sword from the purse, or the power of executing from the power of enacting laws."[23]

The Framers' denial to the president of unilateral authority to conduct foreign policy was illuminated by Hamilton in *Federalist No. 75*:

> The history of human conduct does not warrant that exalted opinion of human virtue which would make it wise in a nation to commit interests of so delicate and momentous a kind, as those which concern its intercourse with the rest of the world, to the sole disposal of a magistrate created and circumstanced as would be a President of the United States.

---

[21] James Madison, "*Federalist No. 51*," in *The Federalist with the Letters of "Brutus,"* ed. Terrence Ball (Cambridge: Cambridge University Press, 2003), 227.

[22] Alexander Hamilton, "*Federalist No. 70*," in The *Federalist with the Letters of "Brutus,"* ed. Terrence Ball (Cambridge: Cambridge University Press, 2003), 341.

[23] Irons, 26.

In *Federalist No. 74*, Hamilton provided the rationale for presidential conduct of war:

> Of all the cares or concerns of government, the direction of war most peculiarly demands those qualities which distinguish the exercise of power by a single hand. The direction of war implies the direction of the common strength; and the power of directing and employing the common strength, forms a usual and essential part in the definition of the executive authority.

Let us turn to Madison for the final word on the war powers in the Constitution. He wrote in 1793, "In no part of the Constitution is more wisdom to be found than in the clause which confides the question of war or peace to the legislature, and not the executive...the trust and the temptation would be too great for any one man."

THE RATIFICATION DEBATE

The *Federalist Papers* served both to explain the content of the new Constitution and as propaganda tool in the ratification debate.

Writing the Constitution was one thing, getting the requisite nine states to ratify the document, quite another. Immediately, opposition formed against the new Constitution. For the sake of understanding, if not pure historical accuracy, we can reduce the post-convention sentiments into two warring camps: The Federalists (such as Hamilton, Madison, and Washington who supported adoption of the Constitution) and the Anti-Federalist (such as George Mason, Elbridge Gerry, Patrick Henry, and Richard Henry Lee, who believed the new Constitution set up too strong a central state with too little democracy in the proposed Constitution).

A highly charged national debate ensued. Literally thousands of essays, editorials, and pamphlets argued the case for and against the proposed Constitution. State Conventions were convened, and the debate over ratification heated up.

Numbered among the Anti-Federalists were some of the most forceful advocates of democracy, Patrick Henry of Virginia (who saw the Federalists as establishing a new "tyranny" writing that the new Constitution "squints towards monarchy"), George Mason also of Virginia, Luther Martin of Maryland, and John Lansing and Robert Yates of New York.

Essentially the Anti-Federalists were a very loose confederation of those who opposed the adoption of the Constitution for a variety of reasons. Many saw the new Constitution as a betrayal of the revolution that undermined the democratic sentiments for which the war was fought. Others saw the Constitution creating a powerful central government that would jeopardize liberty. Still others feared that the president might become too powerful. Some saw the power of the states jeopardized. But the one issue that seemed to unite all opponents to the Constitution was the absence of a Bill of Rights.

Reassuring a skeptical citizenry that indeed this new Constitution *did not* create a new monarchy was one of the chief tasks of the Federalists. Hamilton's *Federalist No. 69* is a direct comparison of the power of the king and the new president. And Hamilton was at pains to convince the public that this new president would not possess the arbitrary and plenary power over war.

Both Madison and Hamilton asserted that the new Constitution was "strictly republican" (*No. 39*), and "wholly and purely republican" (*No. 73*), and would seek "a Republican remedy for the diseases most incident to Republican Government" (*No. 10*).

We often think of separation of powers, and checks and balances as going together. Actually, they are often at odds with one another. Separating power gives each branch its own sphere of power, yet checks and balances require sharing of powers such that one branch may block or check another. Separate or blended? Both, actually. And as the separation and blending are not always clearly defined, political battles between the three branches often occur.

Interaction, cooperation, and syncopation of the branches is required if the government is to legitimately act. And if one branch strongly objects, it may be able to check or veto the others. There is thus a conservative bias toward negative power, or the status quo built into the Constitution. It is easier to block, to preserve the status quo than to initiate change.

For Madison, separation and checks work to balance power. In *Federalist No. 48*, he writes that "unless these departments [the three branches] be so far connected and blended [that does not sound like 'separation'] as to give each a constitutional control over the others [checks], the degree of separation ... essential to free government ... can never in practice be duly maintained [balanced]."

This idea of separation derives mainly from the writings of French philosopher Montesquieu, whose 1748 work, *The Spirit of the Laws* had a profound impact on the Framers. It is also found in John Locke's *Second Treatise on Civil Government* (1690). Madison pays tribute to Montesquieu's influence in *Federalist No. 47*, referring to him as "the oracle who is always consulted and cited on this subject." The centrality of separating powers to the goal of good government is paramount for Madison, as he notes in *Federalist No. 48* that concentrating powers "in the same hands is precisely the definition of despotic government."

Checks and balances are implied in the structure of government established by the Framers, and the words "checks and balances" are nowhere mentioned in the Constitution and appear in the *Federalist Papers* only once (*No. 9*), and in a very narrow sense. In *No. 51*, Madison argues that ambition must check ambition and that power must check power, but he adds that in a republic, the legislature predominates—no balance there.

Madison's goal was to reach a type of Newtonian equilibrium or balance between the branches. Intended to give each branch "the means [powers] and motives [ambition]" to check the others, a rough balance may prevent tyranny.

A separation-of-powers system created three distinct yet interconnected branches of government: Legislative, Executive, and Judicial. They would be separated in primary function, but needed to be connected in the development of policy. No one branch fully controlled another. If one branch encroached into the territory of another, it was in the self-interest of that wronged branch to vigorously defend its power. To again quote Madison, "Ambition must be made to counteract ambition."

In order to legitimately exercise political authority, the actions of government had to be based in the rule of law—a revolutionary concept in its day, and a difficult standard of behavior even in our time. In doing this, the Framers turned the government upside down. The England from which they revolted had the people serving the government, and the king asserting a divine right to be the lawgiver—his will was law. But the Framers made government the servant of the people based not on the whim of one man, but on the collective wisdom of the people as filtered through their representatives and embodied the law. It was ideally to be a government of laws, and not of men. And the supreme law was to be a Constitution.

It was—and is—a difficult requirement imposed on government, as events following the September 11, 2001 terrorist attack against the

United States—as but one of the many examples one could cite—suggests. Some discretion is necessary, as laws cannot account for every contingency. But if this is a high hurdle, it represents an ideal that can never fully be reached.

What theory or style of government does the *Federalist* promote? The mechanisms of *republicanism* and *separation* are clear, but what *brand of politics* is mobilized by the mechanism?

For government to work effectively, bargains, compromises, coalitions, give and take, and in short—*politics*, is necessary. The Framers were both idealists as well as realists, pragmatic as well as hopeful. They sought balance and counterbalance, equilibrium and stability. They were not too trusting in human nature, yet not so cynical as to close the door on popular participation. They understood both the light and the dark sides of human nature, and created a government that could act, but only when there was a broad consensus. It was a cautious government, not one empowered to bold action.

They separated and blended power in a republican framework and institutions so that one-man could not command full power. Checks on power and ambition were designed to bring about agreement, consensus, and moderation.

Was This a New Science of Politics? In creating this new system of government did the Framers (Madison in particular) create "a new science of politics?" In a way, the Framers, to defend their new constitution, had to rely on a new language of politics. Not of power but of checks, representation, election, balances, separation, equilibrium, blending of authority, constitutions, and law.

Drawn as much from the revolution in physics by Newton as from ancient tomes of politics, this new science, mimicking the physical world, spoke of equilibrium and balance. The Framers looked to philosopher David Hume whose essays "That Politics May be Reduced to a Science," published between 1741 and 1752, pointed the way. And while loathe to admit it, the political realism of Machiavelli also played a large part in the development of this new science.

Recognizing that men were not angels, and that ambitions and self-interest dominated, the new science sought to set power against power, ambition against ambition in a search for the ultimate *balance*. Power was to be limited by the rule of law, balanced by checks, and separated in different functional institutions. The result: *equilibrium*.

THE RISE OF PRESIDENTIAL POWER

"I make American foreign policy," said President Harry S Truman. And while this statement may be a bit overstated, Truman was certainly onto something. While the Constitution established a shared model of policy-making, over time presidents have grabbed, and Congress has often willingly given to presidents, a wide range of power over foreign affairs and war.

In the early republic, presidents maintained a semblance of fidelity to the constitutional design of foreign policy making. But over time, wars, crises, the rise of the United States as a world military and economic power served to centralize power under the presidency. After World War II with the rise of the Cold War National Security State, and after 9/11 with the rise of the Anti-Terrorism State, power was further centralized under a powerful and in some ways, Imperial Presidency.

The president of today is clearly the chief architect of American foreign policy. While a president shares some of that power with others, no one is better positioned to influence events and exert leadership than the president. The president is the head of state, chief communicator with the public and other nations, is the nation's chief executive, its commander in chief, and top diplomat.

The president of course, is not alone. All presidents have advisers, cabinets, the CIA, NSA, Foreign Service officers, and a host of others to assist them in developing policy. But the president sits atop this vast collection of diplomats, agencies, and organizations.

The Congress is constitutionally empowered to pass all laws, declare war, confirm treaties, raise armies, appropriate funds, develop policies, and investigate governmental actions. Thus, they have ample power and opportunity to influence foreign policy. So why don't they?

In several key respects, Congress has abdicated its constitutional responsibility in the making of U.S. foreign policy and ceded or delegated vast swaths power to the presidency. Most members of Congress are more concerned with domestic affairs; Congress seldom initiates policies in foreign affairs, and Congress has nearly relinquished its war declaring responsibility to the president.

Over time, the Judiciary has had sporadic involvement in foreign affairs. When it has been involved, it has often allowed the president to grab power. Judicial review of presidential activities in foreign affairs has been infrequent. In fact, scholars Grossman and Wells suggest that, referring to Supreme Court review of presidential foreign policy matters: "In no area of public law has judicial self-restraint been more marked." They go on to give a litany of Supreme Court hesitancy when reviewing foreign policy matters, among them the manner in which treaties are loosely interpreted so as to avoid constitutional conflict; refusal to subject the Congress' "plenary" power over aliens, immigrations, and the acquisition of territory, to more than the "barest procedural requirements"; legitimization of the expanse of presidential power with approving referred to "executive prerogative"; and their reference to the lack of force of the separation-of-powers doctrine when dealing with foreign affairs (as opposed to domestic affairs where the separation doctrine was valid and enforceable on many occasions). Grossman and Wells note that, by recognizing the "very delicate, plenary and exclusive power of the President as the sole organ of the federal government in the field of international relations," the Justices have converted a fact of life into constitutional principle.[24]

This "fact of life" *qua* constitutional principle says, in short, that due to the "unique" constitutional arrangements, foreign policy is political in nature and it was the president, who would be deemed responsible for the conduct of the nation's foreign policy. And as scholar Louis Henkin wrote, "Foreign policy remains very much a political rather than a legal creation and institutional powers and tensions rather than constitutional principle are its dominant determinants."[25]

Thus the Court will often allow for presidential activities in foreign affairs with few limitations.[26] The power to review presidential activities, so potentially potent a weapon under the domestic rubric, becomes somewhat shallow when confronted by the foreign policymaking powers of the president. The Supreme Court, in *Chicago and Southern Air Lines vs.*

---

[24] Joel D. Grossman and Richard S. Wells, *Constitutional Law and Judicial Policy Making* (New York: John Wiley & Sons, 1972), 566. See also: Michael A. Genovese, *The Supreme Court, the Constitution, and Presidential Power* (University Press of America, 1980).

[25] Louis Henkin, "Constitutional Issues in Foreign Policy," *Journal of International Affairs*, Vol. 23, No. 2, (1969), 224.

[26] During the presidency of George W. Bush, the Supreme Court did issue a series of rebellions against the administration (Rasul, Haman, Handi, Bourmedieire) about which we will review later.

Waterman S.S. Corp. said that a president's decisions in foreign policy affairs will rarely be questioned because there are, "...decisions of a kind for which the judiciary has neither aptitude, facilities nor responsibility which have long been held to belong to the domain of political power not subject to judicial intrusion or injury."[27]

A key advantage in the hands of the president is the ability to *initiate* action, striking, acting, and then leaving it to Congress to react. This ability to make the first move gives the executive a major advantage—especially when, as President Obama did in December 2014, in relaxing relations with Cuba, the president surprises Congress and his adversaries. The president may not possess all the Constitutional cards, but the office certainly possesses the political cards to lead.

The problem with the war declaring/authorizing power was again revealed in early 2015 when President Obama—who had been commanding troops in the war against ISIS for months—finally asked the Republican controlled Congress to step up to the plate and grant him authorization to conduct a war he was already conducting.

On February 11, the administration sent to Congress, a draft of war authorization. The Congress was absolutely flummoxed about how to respond. To some in Congress, personal and partisan contempt for President Obama ran so high that they simply refused to give the president authority to wage war—this in spite of railing against the president for *not* being tough enough on the enemy. For others, the prospect of yet another American-led war in the Middle East with U.S. boots-on-the-ground brought out war weariness. To still others, there was confusion in the details of authorizing military engagement.

As many Republicans claimed that Obama was asking for too much authority, House Speaker John A. Boehner (R., Ohio) complained that the president wasn't asking for enough. Boehner called the president's proposal "the beginning of the process," and that three different house committees would hold "extensive hearings" on the proposal.[28] So, as bombs flew and body counts mounted, Congress would hold exhaustive hearings. Congress couldn't lead, wouldn't follow, and didn't get out of the way.

---

[27] Ibid.

[28] Katherine Skiba, "Obama's War Powers bid Disappoints GOP," *Los Angeles Times*, February 16, 2015, A9.

EARLY PRACTICE: THE WAR POWERS IN ACTION

Examining the debate within the Constitutional Convention, the *Federalist Papers* defense of that Constitution, the ratification debate, all help us understand the intent of the Framers. Also, looking at the early practice of the war powers by the men of that era may further illuminate the design for war and peace.

The actual practice of executive dominance in foreign affairs began with the first president, George Washington.[29] From the Neutrality Proclamation in 1793, which Robert Jones calls, "...a significant precedent supporting the idea that the President was the chief author of American foreign policy,"[30] to the Jay Treaty in 1796, Washington established a principle of executive superiority if not supremacy in foreign affairs which has extended into the modern period.

The foreign policy debate during Washington's time took place over the Neutrality Proclamation in conflict, and centered on the Hamiltonian (writing under the pseudonym Pacificus) strong foreign policy president versus the Madisonian (writing as Helvidicus) separation-of-powers model. The proclamation announced the intention of the United States to "pursue a course friendly and impartial to both belligerent powers." Hamilton defended the proclamation and sought to lay out a version of a president who dominated the foreign policymaking process. Madison argued for a more balanced approach, one that did not cede so much unilateral authority to the executive. History has seen the Hamiltonian model thrive while Madison's more moderate model only infrequently shows its face.

The Barbary Wars[31] of the early 1800s raised several key war powers questions. For years, pirates, with the blessing and often at the orders of dey, emperor, sultan, or pasha, of Tripoli, Algiers, Morocco, or Tunis would capture ships (mostly European) and either ransom the officers or sell the crew into slavery, steal the ship, and interfere with trade

---

[29] See: Robert F. Jones, "George Washington and the Establishment of a Tradition," in *Power and the Presidency*, ed. Phillip C. Dolce and George H. Skau (New York: Charles Scribner's Sons, 1970), 13–24.

[30] Ibid., 19.

[31] There were actually two Barbary Wars, the first was the Tripolitan War (1801–1805), the second the Algerian War (1815–1816).

throughout the Mediterranean Sea. Most European nations paid the pirates/nations huge sums of money not to tamper with their ships and crews, believing the cost was less onerous than war.

When the United States won independence, it too had to figure out a way to fend off the pirates. The new nation, in debt, with no standing army or navy, had few options. Both Presidents George Washington and John Adams agreed to pay the pirates, but when Thomas Jefferson became president, the young nation took a different approach. He wanted to fight.[32]

Jefferson had several options: go to Congress and ask for a formal declaration of war; get some sort of authorization from Congress short of a formal declaration of war; commence the fight as the Barbary states had already declared war against the United States, thus a state of war already existed (the Barbary states presumed a state of war until an affirmative treaty of peace—and payment—was signed); act on his own claimed authority as commander in chief absent congressional authorization; or order ships into harm's way and wait to be attacked and then respond with force.

Jefferson, within days of his first inauguration (March 23, 1801), and without Congress, ordered four U.S. warships to sail off the coast of Northwest Africa, and attack ships from any Barbary state that was at war with the United States.[33]

After ordering warships to sail to the Mediterranean, Jefferson had second thoughts and consulted with his cabinet. "Shall the squadron now at Norfolk be ordered to cruise in the Mediterranean? What shall be the object of the cruise?" asked Jefferson. The cabinet agreed that force might be needed to protect U.S. ships. Attorney General Levi Lincoln suggested that the United States take defensive measures if they were attacked, but cautioned against an offensive mission that initiated conflict. Treasury Secretary Albert Gallatin asked if congressional approval might be necessary. Congress was in recess and it would take weeks to assemble. Gallatin argued that the president need not go to Congress as war had already been declared against the United States, thereby creating a state of war to which the president could respond.[34]

---

[32] See: Joseph Wheelan, *Jefferson's War* (New York: Carroll & Graf, 2003); Frank Lambert, *The Barbary Wars* (New York: Farrar, Straus and Giroux, 2007).

[33] Ibid., Prologue and pp. 2–6.

[34] Ibid., 4–5 and Lambert, 123–137

But Jefferson continued to second-guess himself. Was he required to go to Congress? In the end, Jefferson relied on presidential prerogative to defend the United States against a country that had already declared war on the United States. After the squadron left the United States (June 2, 1801), Jefferson formally informed Congressman Wilson Cary Nicholas of the mission.

In the end, Jefferson ordered the squadron to engage any Barbary vessel that interfered with U.S. shipping, but not to pursue or initiate military engagements. Jefferson later went to Congress and received formal authorization to engage solely in defensive military action. Then on February 6, 1802, Congress authorized the president to use all means necessary to defeat the Barbary enemy. Although not a formal declaration of war, it was Congress clearly giving the president the green light for military action.

In the lead up to the Civil War, the new president James Buchanan had a vexing problem with war powers. Several states were on the road to secession. What was he to do? Did he have the authority to use force to quell the rebellion, or must he wait for Congressional authorization? While arguing that succession was against the Constitution, Buchanan nonetheless believed himself to be powerless in the face of the wave of secessions that were on the horizon. He is regarded as one of the worst presidents in history largely due to his passive approach to the crisis of succession.

Abraham Lincoln, on the other hand, acted, and acted boldly. But did he act legally?

Where Buchanan hesitated, Lincoln acted. He did not call Congress into session but acted on his own, suspending *habeas corpus*, put civilians on trial in military courts, raised an army, and militarily engaged the rebellious South.

Several of Lincoln's actions were challenged in the courts. In 1863, in the *Prize Cases*, the Court upheld Lincoln's blockade of southern ports on the ground that he was repelling an invasion pursuant to his authority as commander in chief of the armed forces.

At other times, the president fared less well on the courts. In 1861, in *Ex parte Merryman* Chief Justice Roger Taney, sitting as a federal circuit court judge ruled against Lincoln's suspension of *habeas corpus*. In *Ex parte Milligan* in 1866, the Supreme Court, in a case decided *after* the end of the Civil War, found Lincoln's use of military courts to try civilians to be unconstitutional as the civil courts were still in operation.

Lincoln himself made no bold claims to plenary presidential war powers, arguing that he acted only out of *necessity* (Congress was not in session) and that all the war powers he employed ultimately belonged not to the president but to Congress, and he went to Congress asking for retroactive approval of the steps he had taken. This "act first, ask for permission later" approach is far from ideal, yet it does recognize that Congress must be involved in war decisions for them to be legitimate.

One of the most contested, cited, and controversial court cases dealing with presidential power is *U.S. v. Curtiss-Wright (1936)*. Congress delegated to the president the right to determine whether or not to sell arms to either or both the parties to the Chaco War between Bolivia and Paraguay. President Roosevelt decided to ban all arms sales. The *Curtiss-Wright* Export Corporation challenged the legality of the delegation of powers to the president. What mattered—or at least lasted— was several pages of dicta written by Justice George Southerland, misusing a quote from Congressman, later Chief Justice John Marshall that the president "is the sole organ of the nation in its external relations." From this, advocates of plenary presidential power in foreign policy and war, insist that indeed, the president—and the president alone—makes U.S. foreign policy. This is a very weak reed on which to hang, but those arguing for unchecked presidential power take what they can find. A careful reading of *Curtiss-Wright*, along with an examination of all the material on questions of presidential authority, yields no such conclusion.[35]

Constitutional scholar Edward S. Corwin wrote of the relationship between the president and Congress over control of foreign policy as an "invitation to struggle." By this he meant that both branches have a constitutional role but it remains unsettled who will actually grab power. History demonstrates that it is usually the president who grabs the power. In no area is this more clearly demonstrated than in the power to make war.[36]

---

[35] For a more detailed examination of *Curtiss-Wright*, see two excellent pieces by Louis Fisher: "President's Game," *Legal Times*, December 4, 2006; and "The 'Sole Organ' Doctrine," Study No. 1, *The Law Library of Congress*, 2006–03236, August 2006.

[36] See: David Gray Adler and Larry N. George, *The Constitution and the Conduct of American Foreign Policy* (Lawrence: University Press of Kansas, 1996). (Adler and George 1996).

The modern understanding of the war powers has evolved (or devolved) into a president-centered understanding in which the president may take the nation into armed conflicts without the express approval of Congress. There is no constitutional basis for this transformation. Yet, if the pendulum has swung to the presidency, the fluid nature of the executive-legislative relationship ensures that a tug of war between the two branches over the war powers will continue.

The rapacious nature of the presidential initiatives in war making in recent years has led to a power struggle over who rightly can commit American forces to war. As president, can one *constitutionally* send American troops into battle absent a congressional authorization? There is some debate on this point, especially in a worldwide and, perhaps, never-to-end "war" against terrorism. The war on terrorism has opened old wounds (from the Vietnam era) and it has created new ones. Some, the *Absolutists*, say that a president is free to determine when and where to send American forces, even without the consent of the Congress. John Yoo, who served in the administration of George W. Bush as deputy assistant attorney general in the Office of Legal Counsel, in his book *The Powers of War and Peace*, argues that "the unitary executive" has the authority to start wars and in unencumbered by the burden of gaining congressional support for his policies. This view seems at odds with the intent of the Framers and the words of the Constitution. At the other extreme you will find the *Literalists*, who take the words of the Constitution literally and argue that **only** the Congress can authorize the sending of American troops into combat. In the middle are the *Balancers*, who believe that the president does have some authority to set defense and foreign policy but that all his actions require congressional approval, either explicit—as in a declaration of war—or implicit, as in granting tacit consent to presidential acts. In an age of terrorism, the president does need some authority to protect the national security, and as long as his policies are placed before the Congress for an up or down vote and as long as the president recognizes that the will of Congress and the rule of law are the final word on war, presidents will and must lead.

In the post-World War II era, the power of the American presidency in the field of foreign policy and war has expanded to the point where we commonly refer to the existence of a "National Security State," at the epicenter of which sits an "Imperial Presidency," referring to an ever strengthened institution propelled by executive hegemony in foreign policy. With the fall of the Soviet Union and the end of the Cold War, the Imperial

Presidency lapsed into brief repose. But after the 9/11 attacks, the Anti-Terrorist State was created and the presidency became Imperial once again.

In fits and starts, with two steps forward, one back, the overall trend has been toward the aggrandizement of presidential power. The trend—although interrupted from time to time—has been toward more independent presidential authority in foreign policy and war.

Two important, yet contradictory events in the Truman years point to the unsteady yet central place of the presidency in war and foreign policy. The first marked a dramatic rise in the claims of independent presidential war-making authority; the second, an effort to link presidential foreign policy making to Congress.

Prior to the 1950s, no president claimed independent, plenary constitutional authority to make war. Even the presidents who acted boldly without Congressional approval went to great pains to concede that only Congress had the authority to take the nation to war. But during the Korean Crisis (aka "war"), President Truman—without Congress—not only took the nation to war, but also claimed that he, the president, had the constitutional authority to do so. It was a game changer.

In June of 1950, President Truman ordered U.S. troops into Korea to stop an invasion of Communist forces from North Korea into the South. He did so without first getting authority from Congress. Citing "treaty commitments," as his guiding authorization along with working the president's authority as commander in chief exercising the "traditional power of the President to use the armed forces of the United States without consulting the Congress,"[37] Truman committed U.S. troops to war.

In 1950, testifying before a joint hearing of the Senate Committee on Foreign Relations and Armed Services, Truman's Secretary of State Dean Acheson claimed plenary presidential authority to commit American forces into combat.

> Not only has the President the authority to use the Armed Forces in carrying out the broad foreign policy of the United States and implementing treaties,

---

[37] Arthur M. Schlesinger, Jr., *The Imperial Presidency* (Houghton Mifflin, 1973), 133. (Schlesinger 1973).

but it is equally clear that this authority many not be interfered with by the Congress in the exercise of power which it has under the constitution.[38]

The second key event marked an effort by the Supreme Court to both limit and define the president's foreign policy/war powers. During the Korean War a labor dispute threatened to shut down the steel industry and jeopardize the war effort. President Truman ordered the Secretary of Commerce to take control of the factory and keep it open.[39]

The Supreme Court in *Youngstown Sheet & Tube Co. v. Sawyer* (1952), held that the president had overstepped his authority. Justice Robert Jackson, in a concurring opinion wrote:

> When the President acts pursuant to an expressed or implied authorization of Congress, his authority is at its maximum, for it includes all that he possesses in his own right plus all that Congress can delegate. In these circumstances, and in these only, may he be said (for what it may be worth), to personify the federal sovereignty. If his act is held unconstitutional under these circumstances, it usually means that the Federal Government as an undivided whole lacks power.

During the war in Vietnam, as public discontent rose, another key war powers debate took place surrounding the creation of War Powers Act of 1973. It was an effort by Congress to compel president to consult with the Congress before taking military action, and to set a time limit on such engagements. President Nixon vetoed the act but Congress managed to scrape together the two-thirds vote necessary to override the veto. While well-meaning, the act has not had the desired outcome and now, many feel that the Act should be scrapped and replaced with the original constitutional understanding that only Congress has the power to declare war.

---

[38] See: Edward Keynes, *Undeclared War: Twilight Zone of Constitution Power* (University Park, PA: The Pennsylvania State University Press, 1982). (Keynes 1982).

[39] See: Marcus, Maeva. *Truman and the Steel Seizure Case: The Limits of Presidential Power* (New York: Columbia UP, 1977). Print.

9/11: Everything Changed

In an emergency, the Congress, the public, and the courts defer to the presidency, and while this is politically so, that does not make it constitutionally permissible. After 9/11, virtually everyone looked to the president for crisis leadership. They deferred to the president, and demanded decisive action. Thomas Jefferson, in an 1810 letter to Caesar A. Rodney, presciently wrote that "In times of peace the people look most to their representatives; but in war, to the executive solely."

In post-9/11 efforts to protect the homeland from terrorist thugs, we may have lost sight of the intentions of the Founders of the American republic and come full circle from a revolution against the British monarchy of King George to the creation of a modern presidency with kingly prerogatives?

Within days of the 9/11 attack, a "rally 'round the flag" sentiment swept the country and transformed the president into a warrior-king. On September 12, 2001, the House of Representative voted 420-1, and the Senate 98-0 to support of resolution authorizing President Bush "to use all necessary and appropriate force against those nations, organizations, or person he determines planned, authorized, committed, or aided the terrorist attacks..." a blank check if ever there was one. By comparison, the 1964 Gulf of Ton kin Resolution, which opened the door for the Vietnam War, passed Congress by a virtually identical vote: 416-0 in the House, and 88-2 in the Senate. When we are most in need vigilant congressional oversight, we seem least likely to get it.

One of the architects of the post 9/11, expansive or unitary conception of presidential war powers is John Yoo. A former lawyer in the Office of Legal Counsel (OLC) in the Justice Department, Yoo is responsible for writing some the most controversial internal memos in the weeks after the 9/11 attack—memos that painted a very broad portrait of presidential dominance in war and foreign policy making. Yoo claimed that the world after 9/11 was "very different" and that the "new threats to American national security, driven by changes in the international environment, should change the way we think about the relationship between the process and substance of the warmaking system." Fair enough. But while we are changing the Constitution as practiced to meet the demands of this new age, we still have the 1787

Constitution in place, and we do grave constitutional damage when we disregard it because it is inconvenient.[40]

Some argue that "[t]he president has independent war making powers as Commander-in-Chief" but such claims are constitutionally questionable. As mentioned earlier, the president's authority as commander in chief begins *after* the Congress declares war or otherwise authorizes the president to engage in military action. Here, the intent of the Framers is quite clear, as is the Constitution. Simply and constitutionally put, presidents possess no independent power to initiate war.

The erosion of the constitutional war power has occurred in three stages. In Stage I (1789–1951), the common understanding and practice was that only Congress could initiate war. This view dominated from 1789 until the early 1950s. Stage II began in the early Cold War era and was championed by the Truman administration with the wholehearted support from a surprising source: Congress. In Stage II (1951–2001), the executive asserted independent, unilateral and *constitutional* power to initiate military action. Stage III (2001–?) began after 9/11. The Bush administration advanced the bold claim that not only is the president authorized to take unilateral military action, but in such cases, the president's actions are *unreviewable* by the other branches of government, making the president's acts quite literally above the law.

And yet, on this the Constitution is perfectly clear. Article I, Section 8 reads, in part: "the Congress shall have power . . . to declare war" and Article II, Section 2 says that: "the President shall be commander-in-chief of the army and navy of the United States, and of the militia of the several states, when called into the actual service of the United States." Thus, Congress decides when we are at war, and the president conducts the war. The president may only repel sudden attacks, not initiate military action. That is precisely why James Madison and Elbridge Gerry persuaded the

---

[40] John Yoo, *The Powers of War and Peace: The Constitution and Foreign Affairs After 9/11* (Chicago: University of Chicago Press, 2005). Pages ix and x. See also: Memorandum opinion from John C. Yoo, Dep'y Asst. Att'y Gen., for Timothy Flaigan, Dep'y Counsel to the President, *The President's Constitutional Authority To Conduct Military Operations Against Terrorists and Nations Supporting Them* (September 25, 2001), Memorandum opinion for Alberto Gonzales, Counsel to the President, *Standards for Interrogation under* 18 U.S. C. 2340-2340A (August 1, 2002).

Constitutional Convention to change the wording of the Constitution from Congress shall "make" to "declare" war.

And Alexander Hamilton drew the distinction between a president, limited by the rule of law, and a king possessing grandeur powers when he wrote in *Federalist No. 69* that the president's authority would amount to nothing more than the supreme command and direction of the military and naval forces, as first general and admiral of the Confederacy; while that of the British king extends to the *declaring* of war and to the *raising* and *regulating* of fleet and armies—all which, by the Constitution under consideration, would appertain to the legislature.

This view held sway for most of our nation's history, and was embraced by virtually all the presidents. It was echoed by a young congressman named Abraham Lincoln, in a letter to a colleague at the outset of the Mexican-American war:

> The provisions of the Constitution giving the war-making power to Congress was dictated, as I understand it, by the following reasons: Kings had always been involving and impoverishing their people in wars, pretending generally, if not always, that the good of all kingly oppressions, and they resolved to so frame the Constitution so that no one man should hold the power of bringing oppression upon us.[41]

President George W. Bush has gone beyond previous presidents in his claims of independent foreign policy and war-making authority. Nineteenth century presidents normally paid deference to the superior authority of the Constitution and Congress in matters of war. Cold-War presidents largely abandoned this view, claiming instead that the Constitution actually granted them broad foreign policy making and war powers. President George W. Bush had advanced presidential power claims yet another step, claiming not only a constitutional authority to act without Congress, but further that his actions as chief executive and commander in chief in times of war are unreviewable by, and beyond the reach of Congress and the courts. These assertions appeared in several confidential White House memos, including the April 2003 "Working

---

[41] Quoted in Francis D. Wormuth and Edwin B. Firmage, *To Chain the Dog of War: The War Power of Congress in History and Law* (Dallas: Southern Methodist University Press, 1986), 58. (Wormuth and Firmage 1986).

Group Report on Detainee Interrogations in the Global War on Terrorism," prepared for Secretary of Defense Donald Rumsfeld. Nearly all the public attention paid to this document focused on efforts to justify the use of torture. Largely overlooked was a five-page section of the Report entitled, "Commander-in-Chief Authority," which asserted ultimate and final presidential power subject only to the president's own judgment and disconnected from the Constitution, the law, and the system of checks and balances. The Report further asserts that the president's commander in chief power allows him to "render specific conduct otherwise criminal, not unlawful."[42]

Some suggest that the Framers of the Constitution envisioned presidential primacy in the conduct of war and foreign affairs. Perhaps. But even granting the existence of "primacy," the Founders never intended to create—and clearly did not create—a presidency that was the "sole organ of power in foreign affairs."

Alexander Hamilton, the Constitutional Convention's chief proponent of a strong executive, recognized the limits imposed on the president, writing in *Federalist No. 75*:

> The history of human conduct does not warrant that exalted opinion of human virtue which would make it wise in a nation to commit interests of so delicate and momentous a kind, as those which concern its intercourse with the rest of the world, to the sole disposal of . . . a President of the United States.

There is thus a difference between what is constitutionally permitted and what is politically viable. If constitutional strictures restrain presidential action, political imperatives seem to give presidents near carte blanche authority to act. By seizing the initiative, by acting, presidents may preempt Congress, compelling it to fall in line behind his policy. If initiative rests with a unitary executive, the multitude that composes Congress is forced to react and only rarely will stand up to presidential actions.

The executive's *adaptive capacity*—the ability to decide and act quickly, and its near monopoly over the gathering and control of information—trumps Congress's adaptation handicap, embodied in its need to laboriously harmonize the Congress's multiple voices before it can agree to take action.

---

[42] Report, 50.

As *Federalist No. 64* and *75* remind us, the presidency has unity, decision secrecy, dispatch, stability of purpose, and special sources of information. Taken together, these are a recipe for executive-driven foreign-policy making power.

While some assert that presidents have always claimed independent power over war, and have acted on those claims, this is simply not so. In the early years of the republic, presidents were painstakingly deferential to the Constitution, Congress, and the rule of law. Even President Lincoln, often cited for his unilateral military actions on the outbreak of the Civil War, never wavered from the view that only the Congress had the authority to decide on questions of war. As Richard Henry Dana Jr. told the Supreme Court on behalf of Lincoln in the *Prize Cases* of 1863, Lincoln's military actions at the start of the Civil War did not arise from "the right to initiate a war, as a voluntary act of sovereignty. That is vested only in Congress," and none of the early presidents claimed "inherent" power to initiate military actions. It was only after World War II that presidents began to claim, and Congress began to cede, independent authority over war.

The rise of America's global power meant the rise of presidential power. When the United States became a world economic, military, and political power, a strong presidency emerged. With World War II, the Cold War, and now the war against terrorism, the modern presidency has been driven and shaped by crises and war. With the United States as the world's only super-power, foreign policy animates and empowers a swollen presidency. But this presidency was invented as a limited institution, grounded by the rule of law and embedded in the checks and balances of a separation of powers. Crises and wars have not changed the wording of the Constitution, but they have altered the political context and thus scope of presidential power.

James Madison issued a warning over 200 years ago when he wrote, "Perhaps it is a universal truth that the loss of liberty at home is to be charged to provisions against danger, real or pretended, from abroad."[43]

If we go abroad in search of demons to destroy, we also sacrifice republican principles at home. As we demand security, we suspend the Constitution. Why give terrorists a victory they could never earn on the battlefield? Why let thugs and bullies dictate our policy? Why dismantle the Constitution? The current surrendering of constitutional safeguards is

---

[43] See: Arthur M. Schlesinger, Jr., *War and the American Presidency* (New York: Norton, 2004), 47.

not all together new. In past wars, the United States has trimmed the provisions of the constitution to suit perceived needs and interests.

INTER ARMA ENIM SILENT LEGES OR FULL CIRCLE AND THE RETURN OF THE KING

In the post-Cold War era, the U.S. groped for a strategic vision to animate its foreign policy. Without an identifiable "enemy" the United States drifted, unsure of itself, of what interest to pursue, in what manner, with what tools, towards what end?

Then early on the morning of September 11, 2001, terrorists attacked the United States. The nation and the world awoke to a new threat, a new enemy, and a new strategic mission.

America refocused its energy and attention to fighting a new and different kind of war, a war against the shadowy forces of international terrorism. September 11 changed both the focus of America's attention and the relative power of its institutions of government. In crisis, the public and Congress look to the president as Savior. The power of the president, so often constrained in normal times, expands dramatically in a crisis.

Shortly after the terrorist attack against the United States, President Bush spoke before Congress of a new war—one against the threat of terrorism. He described "a lengthy campaign, unlike any other we have ever seen." This was a war against a stateless shadowy enemy. The president asked for new, expanded powers to deal with this new threat. He also called for and received dramatic increases in defense spending. Between 2001 and 2006, the military budget grew by 39 percent. In 2001, the U.S. military expenditures were $325 billion; the same as the next 14 biggest world militaries combined. By 2005, the United States was outspending the next 14 world militaries by $116 billion.

In the aftermath of the September 11 attacks, the world was overwhelmingly in America's corner. In an editorial in the French newspaper, *Le Monde*, publisher Jean Marie Colombian expressed the sentiments of much of the world when he wrote, "Nous Sommes Tous Americans" ("We are all Americans"). This astonishing burst of pro-American support was reflected in a variety of ways. Italy's *Corriere della Stella* opined, "We are all Americans. The distance from the United States no longer exists because we, our values, are also in the crosshairs of evil minds." And rhetoric was matched with policy. In Brussels, the nineteen ambassadors to the NATO countries invoked, for the first time in its fifty-two year history, Article V of the North Atlantic Treaty, which states that "an armed attack against one or more of them in Europe or North America shall be considered an attack against them all." They further promised concerted action, "including the use of armed forces."

After a halting start, President Bush set in motion a series of policies designed to counterattack the terrorists. The United States assembled an international coalition mobilized to fight terrorists, received enabling authorization from the United Nations and U.S. Congress to go after the enemy, and went to war against the Taliban government in Afghanistan, a protector of the Al Qaeda terrorist cells and supporters of their leader, Osama bin Laden. The initial steps of the war ended quickly and successfully, overthrowing the Taliban government in Afghanistan and weakening Al Qaeda. But only a few years later, the Taliban resurfaced, and fought a guerilla war against America and coalition forces for control of Afghanistan.

After the initial victory in Afghanistan, the president set his sights on another target—Iraq. The war against terrorism was seen in the Bush administration as a way to achieve one of its pre-9/11 goals: to invade Iraq and depose Saddam Hussein. Long a thorn in the side of the West, President Bush's father launched a 1991 war against Iraq to remove it from Kuwait. But the senior Bush stopped short of marching into Iraq and overthrowing Hussein, fearing that the chaos that might follow would be worse than leaving a weakened, defanged Hussein in power. The younger Bush saw his father's mistake. The son would end what the father started. Almost immediately after the 9/11 attack, the Bush administration began planning an attack against Iraq.

What rationale could persuade the public that the war against Al Qaeda should be put on hold to overthrow Iraq? The administration made several arguments—most of them proved to have been unfounded: Hussein was linked to Al Qaeda, said some administration officials; Iraq was sponsoring terrorism, said others; Some said that Hussein had weapons of mass destruction (WMDs) and was a threat to the United States; each of these reasons crumbled beneath the weight of the evidence. Then, the administration developed new reasons: Hussein was a bad man, a Hitler; he was a threat to his own people, and that he was in violation of UN resolutions. Then, when these reasons proved unpersuasive, the administration embraced a version of idealist interventionism ambitious in its scope and violent in execution: it was a war to bring democracy to the Middle East.

All reasons and rationales aside, the Bush administration decided early in their first term that it wanted to overthrow Saddam Hussein.[44] But how to launch an unprovoked attack against another nation? The United States went to the United Nations hoping to receive an empowering resolution as a road to war, but the UN balked at the president; so the United States developed a new strategic doctrine, the "Bush Doctrine," that condoned preemptive and/or preventative war. This "first strike" policy caused an uproar at home and abroad.

On September 20, 2001, President Bush said, "Tonight, we are a country awakened to danger and called to defend freedom. Our grief has turned to anger and anger to resolution...I know there are struggles ahead and dangers to face. But this country will define our times, not be defined by them." These words, spoken before a joint session of Congress, marked the beginning of the president's effort to define his times and impose his imprint on U.S. foreign policy.

The president's rhetoric took on a force that resonated powerfully with the American public. He identified an "axis of evil" (Iran, Iraq, and North Korea) that threatened the United States and promised to back his verbal assault with action. Bush then attempted to build national support to overthrow Saddam Hussein in Iraq. Bush then announced that in the war against terror, one was either with the United States, or with the terrorists. But the overwhelming sympathy and support of the United States in the aftermath of 9/11 and in the war against Afghanistan and Al Qaeda evaporated when President Bush made it clear that Iraq was the next military target.

The president made the case against Iraq, but to critics, fears that the president had "misinformed" the public and Congress about Iraq's supposed efforts to purchase nuclear materials from an African nation, about Iraq's alleged development of weapons of mass destruction and about its supposed role in sponsoring terrorism and Al Qaeda, left suspicion and doubt. The president's case was not convincing to most of the nation's allies.

---

[44] See: Michael A. Genovese, "Bush vs Bush," Paper presented at Hofstra University Conference on the Presidency of George W. Bush, March 2015.

The president was determined to strike Iraq, but Bush faltered badly. Unable to coax an enabling resolution out of a divided United Nations, and unable to build a significant international coalition against Iraq, the president, along with Great Britain and a few other nations, went ahead, and overthrew the government of Iraq in 2003. But the early victory turned to disappointment as the situation in Iraq worsened and civil war developed. Also, an international backlash against the United States followed immediately. Polls demonstrated an overwhelming opposition across to U.S. policy in Iraq, and suspicions that America had used its power inappropriately.

The initial invasion of Iraq ended quickly and with much fanfare. Saddam Hussein was removed from power, eventually captured, put on trial, and hung. The search for WMDs proceeded.

But no WMDs were found, and soon U.S. liberation turned into occupation, and armed resistance in Iraq increased as sectarian violence spread. On May 1, 2003, President Bush flew in a fighter jet onto the deck of the USS Lincoln and delivered a dramatic victory speech in which he declared with a huge banner behind him reading MISSION ACCOMPLISHED that the military portion of Iraq was over. But the war was hardly over, and in the ensuing years of war Americans continued to die by the thousands and Iraq degenerated into civil war.

Then, in early May of 2004, photos were released showing U.S. troops humiliating, sexually degrading, and torturing Iraqi prisoners in the Abu Ghraib prison in Iraq. The photos were grotesque, with American soldiers humiliating prisoners and forcing them to mimic sexual acts upon each other. These pictures caused an uproar at home and abroad, and undermined the claims of moral superiority touted by the Bush administration. Everything began to fall apart in Iraq.

REVOLUTION IN POLICY

The initial military response to the terrorism attack against the United States was only the beginning. President Bush used this opportunity to devise a new—some said revolutionary—approach to the relationship of the United States to the world.

The most significant shift was in the overall strategic approach of the United States toward the rest of the world, in general, and to suspected enemies in particular. The Bush administration, arguing that this new world required new policies, imposed a preventive/preemptive war approach to dealing with problems.

The president declared an international war against a new enemy, terrorism; the U.S.A. Patriot Act was passed by Congress; the Department of Homeland Security was established, a war against the Taliban government in Afghanistan began, the Al Qaeda terrorist network was pursued, a war against Saddam Hussein in Iraq took place. But perhaps more significantly, the administration developed a new strategic doctrine: *First Strike*.

In September 2002, the administration released a national security strategy document that opened with, "The major institutions of American national security were designed in a different era to meet different requirements. All of them must be transformed."

And transform they did. This document describes a fundamentally new, even revolutionary approach to the use of military power internationally. Deterrence and containment, the core doctrines of U.S. power for fifty years during the Cold War, were replaced with doctrines of preemptive and preventative warfare.

This new, more proactive approach was signaled a few months earlier when, at a graduation speech at West Point on June 1, 2002, President Bush, gave a glimpse of what would become the Bush Doctrine. Its merits quoting at some length:

> In defending the peace, we face a threat with no precedent. Enemies in the past needed great armies and great industrial capabilities to endanger the American people and our nation. The attacks of September the 11th required a few hundred thousand dollars in the hands of a few dozen evil and deluded men. All of the chaos and suffering they caused came at much less than the cost of a single tank. The dangers have not passed. This government and the American people are on watch, we are ready, because we know the terrorists have more money and more men and more plans.
>
> The gravest danger to freedom lies at the perilous crossroads of radicalism and technology. When the spread of chemical and biological and nuclear weapons, along with ballistic missile technology—when that occurs, even weak states and small groups could attain a catastrophic power to strike great nations. Our enemies have declared this very intention, and have been caught seeking these terrible weapons. They want the capability to blackmail us, or to harm us, or to harm our friends—and we will oppose them with all our power.

For much of the last century, America's defense relied on the Cold War doctrines of deterrence and containment. In some cases, those strategies still apply. But new threats also require new thinking. Deterrence—the promise of massive retaliation against nations—means nothing against shadowy terrorist networks with no nation or citizens to defend. Containment is not possible when unbalanced dictators with weapons of mass destruction can deliver those weapons on missiles or secretly provide them to terrorist allies. . . .

Homeland defense and missile defense are part of stronger security, and they're essential priorities for America. Yet the war on terror will not be won on the defensive. We must take the battle to the enemy, disrupt his plans, and confront the worst threats before they emerge. In the world we have entered, the only path to safety is the path of action. And this nation will act.

Our security will require the best intelligence, to reveal threats hidden in caves and growing in laboratories. Our security will require modernizing domestic agencies such as the FBI, so they're prepared to act, and act quickly, against danger. Our security will require transforming the military you will lead—a military that must be ready to strike at a moment's notice in any dark corner of the world. And our security will require all Americans to be forward-looking and resolute, to be ready for preemptive action when necessary to defend our liberty and to defend our lives . . .

All nations that decide for aggression and terror will pay a price. We will not leave the safety of America and the peace of the planet at the mercy of a few mad terrorists and tyrants. We will lift this dark threat from our country and from the world . . .

President Bush's first strike/preemptive war doctrine, when joined to his "either you're with us or against us" approach and his willingness to "go it alone" when allies balked at his military ventures, have led to what is referred to as "unilateralism" in foreign policy. This frustrated our traditional allies, just when the United States most needed their help in the global war against terrorism. A nation can pursue its foreign policy interests unilaterally (alone), bilaterally (between two nations) or multilaterally (involving many nations). The President was signaling a willingness to go it alone where necessary, a policy that proved exceedingly costly in lives and treasure in Iraq.

The reaction against the United States was staggering, especially when one considers how overwhelming the support was for the United States in the immediate aftermath of the September 11 attacks. The response from traditional allies was difficult to ignore. A deep vein of global resentment was stuck. Clearly, the new strategic approach employed by the United States was engendering resentment across the globe.

In what came to be known as the "Bush Doctrine," the United States, while perusing diplomatic solutions, announced its right to engage in a preemptive military strike against presumed threats. The President, in short, could declare and start war. Such strikes may—with Iraq—involve a "coalition of the willing," but the United States would not be bound by international organizations such as the United Nations or NATO, and would—when necessary—act alone. Such a doctrine seemed to make a mockery of the Constitutional constraints of the war powers.

This preemptive approach is a proactive, not reactive policy. It seeks to shape and control events, not be shaped by them or act after the fact. At his speech at West Point in June of 2002, President Bush declared, "We must take the battle to the enemy, disrupt his plans and confront the worst threats before they emerge." And "In the new world we have entered, the only path to peace and security is the path of action," reads part of the Bush administration's National Security Strategy Statement, and "the United States cannot remain idle while dangers gather . . . we cannot let our enemies strike first." The Statements further asserted a sweeping universalist declaration of U.S. superiority of ideology when it insists that "our" ideas are "right and true for every person, in every society." And while the administration admitted that this policy held some risks, it also promised results: "The greater the threat, the greater the risk of inaction—and the more compelling the case for taking antiparticipatory action to defend ourselves, even if uncertainty remains as to the time and place of the enemy's attack," said the president. And who would decide when a potential threat merited a military response? The president.

This "new" interpretation of the president's war power spawned an animated debate over the scope and limits of presidential power.[45]

The Framers of the U.S. Constitution believed power in one person's hands would invariably lead to corruption and abuse. The very framework of the government they created—the separation of powers—is testimony

---

[45] See, for example: Jack Goldsmith, *The Terror Presidency: Law and Judgement Inside the Bush Administration* (Norton, 2009); and James P. Pfeffner, *Power Plays: The Bush Presidency and the Constitution* (Brookings, 2009).

to their suspicions about human nature and power in the hands of one person or branch of government. A system of checks and balances would, the Framers hoped, diminish the chances that one man could assume too much power.

And while candidate Obama sounded a retreat from the Imperial Presidency, his behavior as president—while issuing a toned down rhetoric—maintained many of the Bush policies. Chris Edelson argues that the Obama administration has found different—less Imperial ways to reach conclusions similar to Bush.[46]

Regarding President Obama, less of the same is still the same. Bush-lite is still Bush. President Bush's troubling legacy has not been terminated by President Obama, merely adjusted.

THINGS CHANGE

In war and foreign policy, the big "break" from past practice came in the post-World War II era, with the rise of the United States as the dominant hegemonic power in the West, and the emergence of the Cold War competition between the United States and the Soviet Union, then the rise of the Anti-Terrorism state. These highly charged events propelled the United States into international power and leadership, and made the United States the great defender of the West. It also led to the perhaps inevitable emergence of an Imperial presidency.

The rise of America's power paralleled the rise of presidential power. It is thus no accident that U.S. hegemony led to a swollen and powerful presidency. As Clinton Rossiter noted, in the 1960s, "leadership in foreign affairs flows today from the president, or it does not flow at all."[47]

If such a state of affairs undermines the separation of powers and checks and balances created by the Framers, on whom should we level the blame?

---

[46] See: Chris Edelson, *Grand Illusion*; See also: Richard Pious, "Prerogative Power in the Obama Administration," *Presidential Studies Quarterly*, June 2011; Robert Spitzer, "Comparing the Constitutional Presidencies of George W. Bush and Barack Obama: War Powers, Signing Statements, Vetoes," *White House Studies*, Fall 2013.

[47] Clinton Rossiter, "The Presidency—Focus on Leadership," in *American Government: Reading and Cases*, 10th edition, ed. Peter Woll (Glenview, IL: Scott, Foresman/Little Brown Higher Education, 1990), 360.

The Framers assumed that individuals hungered for power. They set up the separation of powers so that when one branch grabbed power, another branch would find it in their interest to grab back. Madison reminded us in *Federalist No. 51*.

> To what expedient, then, shall we finally resort, for maintaining in practice the necessary partition of power among the several departments, as laid down in the Constitution? The only answer that can be given is, that as all these exterior provisions are found to be inadequate, the defect must be supplied, by so contriving the interior structure of the government as that its several constituent parts may, by their mutual relations, be the means of keeping each other in their proper places ...
>
> In order to lay a due foundation for that separate and distinct exercise of the different powers of government, which to a certain extent is admitted on all hands to be essential to the preservation of liberty, it is evident that each department should have a will of its own; and consequently should be so constituted that the members of each should have as little agency as possible in the appointment of the members of the others ...
>
> But the great security against a gradual concentration of the several powers in the same department, consists in giving to those who administer each department the necessary constitutional means and personal motives to resist encroachments of the others. The provision for defense must in this, as in all other cases, be made commensurate to the danger of attack. Ambition must be made to counteract ambition. The interest of the man must be connected with the constitutional rights of the place. It may be a reflection on human nature, that such devices should be necessary to control the abuses of government. But what is government itself, but the greatest of all reflections on human nature? If men were angels, no government would be necessary. If angels were to govern men, neither external nor internal controls on government would be necessary. In framing a government which is to be administered by men over men, the great difficulty lies in this: you must first enable the government to control the governed; and in the next place oblige it to control itself. A dependence on the people is, no doubt, the primary control on the government; but experience has taught mankind the necessity of auxiliary precautions.

In effect, the president is behaving precisely as Madison anticipated; looking for opportunities and openings to grab power. It is the Congress that is not doing its job! Congress has not lived up to its part of the constitutional bargain. It has not met ambition with ambition; it has delegated or ceded to the presidency powers that rightfully belong to it. Yes, blame the presidents for their rapacious power appetites, but blame too the lack of will and spine of the Congress.

THE PRESIDENCY, FOREIGN POLICY, AND WAR

As demonstrated, the Framers attempted to build a shared model of political decision making into their new constitutional republic. How has the presidency come to so dominate decisions relating to war and foreign policy?

The answer to that question is a long, involved story, grounded in history, the rise of the United States as a world economic and military power, war, and crises, the institutional/structural designs of the executive, and disputes over constitutional powers.

In this and all struggles, the Constitution must be our starting point. What was the "original intent" of the Framers? Modern neo-conservatives often demand that an original intent test be imposed in constitutional questions, yet they are either reluctant to apply this test to war powers, or they, cherry-picks the data, employing only those few selected bits and pieces that support their position of expansive presidential authority in war.[48] But any comprehensive and fair-minded examination of the Framers original intent on war, an examination that attempts to take into consideration *all* the evidence, not merely those bits that support a particular preordained outcome, must come away with the conclusion that

(a) The making of foreign policy was the shared responsibility of the president and Congress.
(b) In what Corwin refers to as the Constitution's "invitation to struggle" for control of foreign affairs, the president is well positioned to lead.
(c) In war, only the Congress is authorized to declare or initiate military action.

---

[48] See: John Yoo, *The Powers of War and Peace* (Chicago: The University of Chicago Press, 2005); and *War By Other Means* (New York: Atlantic Monthly Press, 2006).

(d) Once declared or authorized, the president, as commander in chief, takes on added authority to conduct or prosecute the war.

(e) During war, the Congress maintains its authority to determine the course of war via the purse, its possession of legislative authority and through oversight.

(f) All presidential actions in wartime are reviewable by both the Congress and the courts.

That is the original intent of the Constitution and that is what the United States is legally required to follow. The making of foreign policy is the joint responsibility of the president and Congress, and while the Constitution does indeed invite a constant struggle for control, both branches have legitimate and constitutional roles to play.

THE POWER OF CONTEXT

"It is chiefly in its foreign relations," wrote Tocqueville in 1851, "that the executive power of a nation finds occasion to exert its skill and its strength." And Tocqueville sounded an alarm that would not fully be realized for a century: If America's "chief interests were in daily connection with those of other powerful nations, the executive government would assume an increased importance in proportion to the measure expected of it and those which it would execute."[49]

Institutionally, presidents have key advantages over Congress in seizing control of foreign policy and war. In effect, the presidency is a "modern" institution, with adaptation capabilities. The Congress is a deliberative body with an adaptation crisis.

The presidency is "modern" in that it is capable of quick movement, flexibility, change, and adaptation. It is a "streamlined" institution in the sense that it can adapt and adjust quickly, and change to meet changing circumstances. In a fast-paced world, the presidency can keep up with change.

The Congress was designed as a deliberative, eighteenth-century body. It moves slowly. In many ways, it is better suited to the eighteenth than twenty-first century. This deliberative nature allows Congress to discuss, debate, bargain, and compromise, but not act swiftly. If decisions need to

[49] Alexis de Tocqueville, *Democracy in America* (New York: 1948), 137–138.

be made the Congress may not be able to keep up. Thus, Congress has an *adaptation crisis*, while the presidency has an *adaptation capability*.

Translated into the realm of power, this means that the presidency can initiate, take action, preempt, move, act, and lead. The Congress can only rarely do so. It often merely reacts to steps the presidents have already taken. Thus, the built-in bias toward presidential leadership gives the president the upper hand in policy making. Often, the Congress is left to react to steps already taken by the president.

This is not to argue that Congress *can't* move quickly. There are times when it does.[50] Sometimes...sometimes. But most of the time it moves painfully slowly. This is also not to argue that quick decisions by unilateral structures are good. Sometimes they are, sometimes, not. A quick decision *may* lead to a good outcome, but it might also be an unchecked decision that leads to disaster.

In war, if the president acts boldly against a perceived threat, the Congress is all but compelled to support the executive, lest they be accused of weakness, or worse, lack of patriotism. This ability to act swiftly boxes the Congress into a reactive corner, as they may be caught by surprise, or left debating while the president is acting.

Two further distinctions must be made at this point: there is a difference between foreign policy and domestic policy; and there is a difference between routine and normal circumstances, and crisis and war.

Let us look at the differentiation between domestic and foreign policy as they relate to the Presidency. Aaron Wildavsky, in his now famous "Two Presidencies" article said that

> The United States has one president, but it has two presidencies; one presidency is for domestic affairs, and the other is concerned with defense and foreign policy. Since World War II, presidents have had much greater success in controlling the nation's defense and foreign policies than in dominating its domestic policies.... In the realm of foreign policy there has not been a single major issue on which presidents, when they were serious and determined, have failed.[51]

---

[50] Chris Edelson and Donna G. Starr-Declan, "Libya, Syria, ISIS, and the Case Against the Energetic Executive," *Presidential Studies Quarterly*, forthcoming.

[51] Aaron Wildavsky, "The Two Presidencies," *Trans-actions*, December 1966, 7–8.

The result is a president with more freedom in foreign policy areas. This leads a president to concentrate more time and energy on foreign policy issues. John Kessel conducted a content analysis of Presidential State of the Union messages and noted the tendency was for greater attention to be paid to foreign policy issues as time in office increased.[52]

Spanier and Uslaner support Wildavsky's two presidencies notion and suggest that in addition to the reason offered by Wildavsky that the Constitution contains what the authors call "missing powers," which lead the president to claim addition "implied powers" in his conduct of foreign policy. This, plus other factors lead Spanier and Uslaner to write:

> Of the two Presidencies, the foreign one is clearly stronger. In the domestic sphere the President has to bargain harder and longer, and Congress, interest groups, and public opinion are not as deferential and willing to accept Presidential policies.[53]

There is, further, a distinction between what is permitted in a crisis or war, versus the limits imposed in normal times. In crisis, tradition calls for the president to step to the forefront and assume command. As the principal actor in foreign policy process, the president, during crisis, is granted and assumes wide ultra-constitutional powers. Clinton Rossiter criticized the separation of powers for its "crisis inefficiencies" and suggested that in a crisis we turn to the president as the "constitutional dictator." Whatever label one cares to place upon the crisis president, it is clear that during crisis, the public, courts, and Congress generally look to the chief executive to assume control.

In a crisis, the president is usually granted a wide breath of powers. These emergency (or prerogative) powers[54] assumed by the president have a variety of justifications. Clinton Rossiter laid out an elaborate rational for emergency presidential power in *Constitutional Dictatorship*,[55] as did Arthur M. Schlesinger Jr. in *The Imperial Presidency*,[56] Richard M. Pious

---

[52] John H. Kessel, *The Domestic Presidency* (Druxbury Press, 1975).

[53] Spanier and Uslaner, op cit, 26.

[54] See: Michael A. Genovese, "Democratic Theory and the Emergency Powers of the President," *Presidential Studies Quarterly* IX, No. 3, (Summer 1979).

[55] Clinton Rossiter, *Constitutional Dictatorship: Crisis Government in the Modern Democracy* (Princeton, NJ: Princeton University Press, 1948). 99, 297–306.

[56] Arthur M. Schlesinger, Jr., *The Imperial Presidency* (Boston: Houghton, 1973). 450–451. (Schlesinger 1973).

in *The American Presidency*,[57] and Robert E. Di Clerico in *The American President*.[58] But, whatever the specific rationale, all agree that during a crisis, the body of politics turns to the president to "save" the political system.

Article II of the Constitution gives the president the executive power, and it was Alexander Hamilton, in *Federalist No. 64* and *75* who saw in this a "structural advantage" for the president. Given *unity, decision, secrecy, dispatch, stability of purpose*, and unique sources of information and communication, the president would likely hold the upper hand in foreign policy decision making. And during war, the presidential advantage was more powerfully drawn. "It is of the nature of war," wrote Hamilton in *Federalist No. 8*, "to increase the executive at the expensive at the expense of the legislative authority."

[57] Richard M. Pious, *The American Presidency* (New York: Basic Books, 1979), 84.

[58] Robert E. Di Clerico, *The American President* (Englewood Cliffs, NJ: Prentice-Hall, 1979), 309–310.

CHAPTER 2

Prescriptions for a New Age

Abstract Here, Michael Genovese presents his agenda to reform the war powers in light of the new demands of a new age. He calls for slightly more presidential authority, and a different form of accountability for the president's decisions on war. Arguing that the eighteenth-century Constitution is not well suited for a twenty-first-century superpower facing the threat of terrorism, Genovese calls for a more muscular presidency, but one still enchained by congressional accountability.

Keywords All the above from Chapter 1, plus · Courts · Supreme Court · Rule of law

WHAT TO DO?

A strict observance of the written laws is doubtless *one* of the high duties of a good citizen, but it is not *the highest*. The laws of necessity, of self-preservation, of saving our country when in danger, are of higher obligation. To lose our country by a scrupulous adherence to written law, would be to lose the law itself, with life, liberty, property, and all those who are enjoying them with us; thus absurdly sacrificing the end to the means.
—Thomas Jefferson Letter to John Colvin, September 20, 1810

For the past thirty years, I have been a *constitutional conservative* regarding the war powers. I have tried to cling to the original vision of the Founders that

© The Author(s) 2017   53
M.A. Genovese, D.G. Adler, *The War Power in an Age of Terrorism*, The Evolving American Presidency,
DOI 10.1057/978-1-137-57931-7_2

gave Congress the authority to plunge the nation into war. That model worked fairly well for over 150 years, but it may no longer serve the vital interests of the nation. The world has changed, the role of the United States in the world has changed, and so too must we to keep up with these monumental changes. It is time to revamp the war powers. And yet, how do we maintain accountability while further empowering the presidency? Herewith, a modest proposal for a twenty-first-century superpower struggling to protect the national security while also ensuring accountable government.

Was it wise for our Founders to place the war declaring powers solely in the hands of the Congress? Was it practical? Was it (is it) dangerous?

We are a twenty-first-century superpower, governed by an eighteenth-century Constitution. In an age of terrorism and hyper-change[1] can we afford to maintain our devotion to the original Constitution, or is it time for a bit of constitutional tinkering?

The rule of law was in many ways a revolutionary concept: the only way the government could legitimately act was on the basis of written law. The will of the king or president was not enough. Governmental actions had to be based on written codes, rules, and agreed upon grants of power.

We may ask: *were they right?* Were they right for *their* time, for *our* time, for *all* time? Did the Constitution work as the Framers planned, hoped, and anticipated? How did the rise of democracy, the emergence of political parties, industrialization, urbanization, growth, and the rise of the media affect our politics and our Constitution? And did the emergence of the United States as a superpower impact the constitutional order? Has America's power outstripped its constitutional design? Have we become too big, too powerful for our Constitution? Does the fast-paced nature of the modern world require a more streamlined (and executive dominated) order?[2] Must an imperial power have an imperial government?

The Constitution cannot be a straightjacket, nor can it be a suicide pact. It must meet the needs of today. Is it doing so?

The United States was established as a constitutional republic, yet we have become a presidential nation.[3] Should we reclaim our place as a constitutional

---

[1] See: Michael A. Genovese, *The Future of Leadership: Leveraged Leadership in an Age of Hyper-Change* (New York: Routledge, 2015).

[2] See: Michael A. Genovese, *The Future of Leadership* (Routledge, 2015).

[3] Michael A. Genovese, *A Presidential Nation* (Westview, 2013).

republic by cutting down to size the scope of presidential power, or admit that the twenty-first century requires strong presidential leadership, and redesign our system to reflect the demands of modernization and hyper-change?

As much as we may wish to go back to the original design and distribution of power in the Framers' constitution, this could only happen if we retreat from global leadership and drastically reduce the size and scope of the federal government. This is unlikely to happen.[4] Yet, in maintaining the fiction that we are still a constitutional republic, bounded by the Constitution of 1787, we are living a lie that does damage to the rule of law. We must open our eyes and admit that in practice we are no longer a constitutional republic but a presidential nation. Further, we must reclaim the rule of law and Constitutionalism by admitting that we need a strong president but one under a regime of democratic accountability and a more streamlined separation-of-powers system that gives the president more legal power yet binds the office in a rejuvenated check and balance regime. In doing this, we can again claim to be guided by constitutional principle, but principles that better suit a modern superpower.[5]

How do we transform our eighteenth-century Constitution into a twenty-first-century document designed for a world superpower, and support presidential power and leadership while we also control and constitutionalize it? Can the presidency be made both powerful *and* accountable?

The president has been handed (the War Powers Resolution) the authority to start, if not declare war (for a limited time period). Perhaps, our first step should be to revoke the War Powers resolution and return to constitutional moorings in the commitment of American forces to war. And perhaps, also, we should pay for the wars we fight (a temporary war tax) and not put the bill on an American credit card to be paid by future generations. To do this, we must reconceptualize an understanding of the president and war in the modern era.

In this we can be guided by the model presented by Clinton Rossiter over half a century ago: "A strong president is a bad President, a curse upon the land, unless his means are constitutional

---

[4] For an examination of the various approaches one might take in reforming the Presidency, see: Michael A. Genovese, ed., *Contending Approaches to the American Presidency* (Washington, D.C.: CQ Press, 2012).

[5] See: Bruce Buchanan, *Presidential Power and Accountability* (Routledge, 2013).

and his ends democratic, unless he acts in ways that are fair, dignified, and familiar, and pursues policies to which a 'persistent and undoubted' majority of the people has given support. We honor the great Presidents of the past, not for their strength, but for the fact that they used it wisely to build a better America."[6] Our goal, as Arthur M. Schlesinger, Jr. reminded us in his book *The Imperial Presidency*, is to "devise means of reconciling a strong and purposeful Presidency with equally strong and purposeful forms of democratic control."[7] He went on to argue that we do need a strong president, but "one within the Constitution."[8]

The Framers established separate institutions that shared powers as "the essential precaution in favor of liberty."[9] Ours is a three-branch system of government and no single branch can eclipse the others in power as to avoid the checks and balances of our system of governing. Yet how do we reinvigorate the system of powers for a modern age? To do this we need both constitutional and political change.

CONSTITUTIONAL CHANGE

An Emergency Constitution?

The Framers did not put into the Constitution any provision for emergency transfers of power to the executive. They could have, as they were familiar with republican Rome's constitution and its provisions under grave emergencies to temporarily turn dictatorial powers over to one man.

Yale's Bruce Ackerman proposes that the United States set up a system wherein during an emergency a temporary dictatorship is created to deal with crisis. This "emergency constitution" would be limited in duration and must meet a set of standards, but it would

---

[6] Clinton Rossiter, *The American Presidency* (New York: Harcourt, Brace and World, 1956), p. 257.

[7] Arthur M. Schlesinger, Jr., *The Imperial Presidency* (Boston: Houghton Muffin, 1973). (Schlesinger 1973).

[8] Schlesinger, Jr., *The Imperial Presidency*. (Schlesinger 1973).

[9] *The Federalist Papers*, No. 47 and 51.

allow for the expansive use of power while not forcing the president to act beyond the law.[10] I do not favor such a proposal.

Reform War Powers

The Constitution is clear: only Congress has the power to declare war. Yet, over time presidents have ignored the Constitution and on numerous occasions ordered American troops into combat.

In the modern world, where the United States serves as the only superpower, can the war power be tamed and brought back under congressional control? Given the importance of the decision to go to war in a nuclear age, it seems vital to put presidential decisions under closer scrutiny and tighter congressional controls.

Of course, Congress *already has* all the constitutional authority it needs to tame the presidency in war. What is lacking is the political will. When presidents grab the war powers, Congress meekly retreats. Where presidents act, Congress hesitates.

Strengthening the War Powers Resolution might help but there is no constitutional or statutory way to instill more institutional or personal backbone into the Congress. If Congress wishes to "chain the dog of war," it already has all the necessary tools. The problem is that these tools are dying of atrophy.

A 2008 commission co-chaired by former Secretary of State James Baker and Warren Christopher wrestled with this complex issue, and offered a proposal for a law entitled the *War Powers Constitutional Act of 2009*. Aimed at correcting the shortcomings of the *War Powers Resolution*, the idea was to strengthen the "consultation" between branches. The proposal also called for a "Joint Congressional Consultation Committee" to facilitate legislative-executive consultation. This idea never got traction, but this report remains a useful addition to the war powers debate.[11]

[10] Bruce Ackerman, *Before The Next Attack* (New Haven: Yale University Press, 2006).

[11] James Baker, Warren Christopher, *Natural War Powers Report* (Washington, D.C., 2008).

Impeachment

No U.S. president has ever been impeached and convicted. Only two have been impeached. This leads some critics to lament that the impeachment process has no teeth.

The bar is—and should be—high regarding impeachments. It is a blunt instrument and should be reserved only for the most grievous of "high crimes and misdemeanors." In an effort to reign in the war-making power of the presidency, we should amend the Constitution to add to the list of "treason, bribery, and other high crimes and misdemeanors," "unauthorized war-making" as another impeachable offensive.

The presidency is broken, and it needs to be fixed. But it isn't *so* broken that we need to perform major surgery. How can we (1) empower the president to govern on a global stage (2) ensure accountability; and (3) protect the rights and liberties so valued by Americans? Reforming the presidency is not enough. We must take an integrated or holistic approach to reform. Herewith, my immodest proposal:

OLD WINE IN NEW BOTTLES JUST WON'T DO: RETHINKING THE WAR POWERS IN AN AGE OF TERRORISM

Political Changes

In 1787, vesting the war powers in the hands of Congress made a great deal of sense. The collective wisdom of society as filtered through representatives, not the will or whim of one man, should guide the republic in this momentous decision. That was then, this is now.

The world is changing rapidly and our eighteenth-century Constitution, which has serves us so well for so many years, simply is not well suited to meet the demands of the twenty-first century.

In the beginning of the republic, Congress—a slow, deliberative body—could discuss and debate issues of war. We no longer always have that luxury. The Framers model worked well for over 150 years. Then, for a variety of reasons, presidents grabbed the war powers and made it their own, in practice if not in law. And Congress was usually a willing bystander in this theft of constitutional authority. Today, for all intents and purposes, presidents "declare" war simply by leading the nation into war. In doing so, in allowing so, we become *constitutional hypocrites*, singing the praises of a constitution we no longer follow. So is it possible to streamline the process and give Congress a key role in war declaring, while also recognizing that our original model does not serve us well today? Can we make presidents powerful yet democratically accountable?

A *Strong Presidency* Needs a Strong Congress, and We Need Both:

Some reformers, believing that a strong presidency is necessary to promote U.S. global leadership, seek to strengthen the check-and-balance system by calling for a strong Congress, but not the Congress as currently structured. A stronger Congress that remains ill-suited to the modern capacity to move quickly would only exacerbate the already debilitating deadlock that so often characterizes the congressional input to policy making. We need a stronger Congress, but also a *different* type of Congress.

Thus, to revitalize Congress, we must *streamline Congress*, brining it out of the eighteenth and into the twenty-first century. The presidency dominates because it can adapt. It can adapt because one hand is at the helm. As currently structured, Congress cannot govern, and it should not govern. If it wants to become relevant in an ongoing manner, Congress must become a modern institution, capable of providing accountability and timely decision-making. Congress must streamline its process by giving greater authority to what is called the Gang of Eight, the top elected leaders from both parties. Today, a small number of activists in Congress can utterly tie up the entire institution, preventing it from conducting necessary business. By granting more authority to the Gang of Eight, the leadership of Congress would be compelled to accept more responsibility and might be able to bypass the gridlock so often displayed in relations between the president and Congress. This is especially important when the war powers are considered. When a president—even in a sudden emergency—feels compelled to put our troops into combat situations, he should be *required* to consult with the Gang of Eight (or six, if necessary).

The congressional process must be streamlined so that a president can more fruitfully consult with Congress. Presidential initiatives must go to the Congress *before* action is taken—even in covert operations—and Congress must establish a *fast-track* decision process to respond to a president in a timely fashion. The president must meet with the Gang of Eight on a regular basis, and this congressional leadership group must have the authority—if it deems it necessary—to authorize or postpone (for up to 48 hours, giving the entire Congress the opportunity to respond) presidential acts while placing the president's plan before a fast-track congressional vote.

This applies not only to war, but to other areas such as covert activities where one needs accountability and timely oversight, but—perhaps—also secrecy and dispatch. The world moves quickly, Congress moves slowly, and there are times when waiting endangers the interests of the nation.

Truncating the process allows the congressional leaders to be consulted *and* have their will executed. If the president, facing congressional leaders who refuse to give him the green light, wishes to take his case to a closed session of the full Congress for an up or down vote (with limited debate, and no amendment or restrictions), the president may do so. This (1) keeps Congress in the mix (2) undermines the president's view that he needs to— for the sake of timelines—by pass Congress (3) gives the president a mechanism with which to act within the spirit of constitutionalism and legitimacy; and (4) forces both branches to work together in developing policy.

Harold Koh calls for the creation of a *core consultative group* in Congress. The benefits of such a group can be seen in its ability to bring Congress into the decision-making process *before*, not after decisions are made and actions taken. As Koh writes: "By first creating a core group of members, with whom the president and his staff could meet regularly and consult on national security matters, Congress could provide the executive with the benefit of its deliberative judgments without demanding unacceptable sacrifices in flexibility, secrecy, or dispatch...The group would have formal authority to invoke the War Powers Resolution even if the president chose not to do so; its legislative proposals would be accorded a special fast-track status in the legislative process."[12] Koh also calls for the creation of a *congressional legal advisory*, giving Congress greater access to executive branch information. And of course Congress must reclaim the war powers.

Congress must be reformed and restructured if it is not merely to play a passive role. Political Scientist Andrew Rudalevige writes, "The critical question, then, is straightforward: why had Congress been so acquiescent? The fact is that we have had an invisible Congress as much as an imperial president. Must of the expansion in presidential power has not been taken but given."[13]

---

[12] Koh, *The National Security Constitution*, 167.

[13] Andrew Rudalevige, *The New Imperial Presidency* (Ann Arbor: University of Michigan Press, 2006), 275.

Congress will remain on the outside looking in if it does not reform itself. The presidency is built for speed; the Congress is built for deliberation. Deliberate it must, but Congress must also find ways to more efficiently *decide*. Until it does, presidents will find ways to bypass or blow past the lethargic legislative branch.

PRESIDENTIAL POWER IN A DANGEROUS WORLD

The powers of the presidency have—absent any constitutional changes—grown dramatically over the years. Without any formal articulation of the expanded presidency, presidents have merely stepped in, acted, and taken power. Historian Arthur M. Schlesinger, Jr., writes that the modern presidency "has come to see itself in messianic terms as the appointed savoir of a world whose unpredictable dangers call for a rapid and incessant deployment of men, arms, and decisions behind a wall of secrecy." He adds, "This seems hard to reconcile with the American Constitution."[14] Congress often turned a blind eye as willing enabler of the demise of its own constitutional powers and at other times, actively delegated its powers to the executive.

With More Power, More Accountability

Can the presidency be strong *and* constitutional? Strong enough to fulfill its constitutional duties yet accountable enough not to pose a threat to our republican values? If the United States is the imperial power, must we also have an imperial presidency? Sadly, in some ways, we seem to have come full circle, from a revolution against the absolute power of a monarch to a presidency that more closely resembles the king than a republican president. Has the imperial presidency become the norm?

Our constitutional system *is* slow in operation. Indeed we *may* need to give more constitutional/legal power to the presidency in the modern age. But we have allowed presidents—usually with the best intentions—to hijack the Constitution and make a shambles of the rule of law. Thus we have the *worst* of both worlds: a powerful presidency above the law, and a deteriorating system of accountability.

[14] Arthur M. Schlesinger, Jr., *War and the American Presidency* (New York: W.W. Norton, 2004), 66.

Bolster the presidency, yes, but bolster also the agencies of democratic accountability. Accountability involves not only responsiveness to majority desires at elections but also taking the Constitution into account day by day. It also suggests a performance guided by integrity and character. Accountability also implies that key decisions be explained to the people allowing them the opportunity to appraise how well a president is handling the responsibilities of the job.

The United States needs a strong presidency and a democratically controlled presidency, a strong presidency and strong citizenship. Benjamin R. Barber notes the difficulty inherent in such a goal:

> At the heart of democratic theory lies a profound dilemma that has afflicted democratic practice at least since the eighteenth century. Democracy requires both effective leadership and vigorous citizenship: yet the conditions and consequences of leadership often seem to undermine civic vigor. Although it cries for both, democracy must customarily make do either with strong leadership or with strong citizens. For the most part, depending on devices of representation in large-scale societies, democracy in the West has settled for strong leaders and correspondingly weak citizens.[15]

James Madison's caution in the *Federalist, No. 51*, speaks volumes to us today: "If men were angels, no government would be necessary. If angels were to govern man, neither external nor internal controls in government would be necessary. In framing a government which is to be administered by men over men the great difficulty lies in this, you must first enable the government to control the government and in the next place oblige it to control itself. A dependence on the people is, no doubt, the primary control on the government. But experience has taught mankind the necessity for auxiliary precautions."

IS THE PRESIDENCY SAFE FOR DEMOCRACY?

Given that the world remains a dangerous place, given that Congress moves slowly, given that the unity and structure of the executive disposes it to act quickly when necessary, we can expect to see presidents,

---

[15] Benjamin R. Barber, "Neither Leaders Nor Followers," in *Essays in Honor of James MacGregor Burns*, eds. Thomas E. Cronin and Michael R. Beschloss (Englewood Cliffs, NJ: Prentice Hall, 1989), 117.

when confronted by grave threats, assume and exercise prerogative and unilateral powers.

But all unilateral acts are not equal. The president may have no constitutional ground on which to act, yet act he must. Therefore, to exercise this power, he must step outside the law and employ extra-constitutional powers. This places a great deal on the shoulders of the president. Not only must he solve the problem, but he must also recognize that he has no strictly legal authority on which to act and must in the end place his actions before the Congress, the courts, and the public for a type of retroactive approval.

If the unilateral presidency is here to stay—a necessary by-product of the slowness of the separation-of-powers system in operation; a recognition that a war against terrorism and other threats may well be with us for a very long time—does that mean we must remain vulnerable to one-man rule? That we must institutionalize an imperial presidency? Does permanent crisis create a permanent imperial presidency? It need not.

CHAPTER 3

The Relevance of the War Clause and the Rule of Law in Our Time

To what purposes are powers limited, and to what purpose is that limitation committed to writing, if these limits may, at any time, be passed by those intended to be restrained?

(Chief Justice John Marshall, *Marbury v. Madison*)[1]

We in America should see that no man is ever given, no matter how gradually, or how noble and excellent the man, the power to put this country into a war.... For when you give power to an executive you do not know who will be filling that position when the time of crisis comes.

(Ernest Hemingway, "Notes on the Next War." Esquire (September, 1935))

Abstract The constitutional grant to Congress—not to the president—of authority to initiate war on behalf of the American people remains adequate to our national security needs in the age of terrorism. The argument for further concentration of power in the president ignores the practice of presidential usurpation of the war power, which has become commonplace, and rests on mistaken assumptions of executive perception, judgment, expertise, and the need for immediate military actions. It ignores as well the fact that unilateral presidential decision-making has resulted in tragic wars. The constitutional

---

[1] "The government of the United States," Marshall wrote in Marbury, "has been emphatically termed a government of laws and not men." 5 U.S. (I Cranch) 137, 163 (1803).

© The Author(s) 2017
M.A. Genovese, D.G. Adler, *The War Power in an Age of Terrorism*, The Evolving American Presidency,
DOI 10.1057/978-1-137-57931-7_3

arrangement on matters of war and peace rightly exalts congressional discussion and debate—collective decision-making—over the judgment of a single person before the nation is plunged into war.

Keywords War clause · War power · Rule of law · Marbury v. Madison · Executive unilateralism (see presidential unilateralism) · Emergency power · Executive power · Federalist papers · Steel seizure case (see Youngstown Sheet and Tube Co. v. Sawyer) · Constitutional convention · Plenary presidential power · Presidential powers · Commander in chief clause · Commander in chief · Vesting clause · Executive power clause · Retroactive ratification · Presidential wars · McCulloch v. Maryland · Articles of confederation · Constitutional design for foreign affairs · Foreign affairs · Use of military force · Helvidius · Presidential war power · Presidential prerogative power · War on terror

The War Clause and the Rule of Law

The 9/11 attack on America has provided yet another circumstance for advocates of executive unilateralism to urge further concentration of power in the president to meet emergencies. Like the Cold War before it, the assertion of a "War on Terror," has been invoked, and exploited, to rationalize presidential acts and claims of power that defy the metes and bounds of the Constitution. The assertion of an emergency, however, does not alter the constitutional allocation of power. In 1935, Chief Justice Charles Evans Hughes stated: "Extraordinary conditions do not create or enlarge governmental power."[2] If it were otherwise, if the president asserted an emergency power coterminous with the emergency that he proclaimed, then his authority, as Justice Robert H. Jackson observed in his landmark opinion in *The Steel Seizure Case*, would have no "beginning or no end."[3] The premise of an illimitable executive power rings hollow in a republic and represents a profound threat to the rule of law but it was, nonetheless, asserted by officials in the administration of George W. Bush. They

[2] *Schechter Poultry Co. v. United States*, 295 U.S. 495, 528.
[3] *Youngstown Sheet and Tube Co. v. Sawyer*, 343 U.S. 579, 646 (1952).

maintained, for example, that Congress may not interfere with the president's sole authority to conduct American foreign policy; that the president, alone, in the exercise of his inherent power, decides what constitutes the nation's security interests and that he, alone, determines when to deploy the nation's armed forces; that the president's foreign affairs actions are not reviewable by the courts, and that constitutional principles are "quaint" in the context of the War on Terror.[4] How was it, we might wonder, that Cicero, some 2000 years ago, could have anticipated conditions in America when he observed that, in times of war and crisis, the "laws buckle"?

There are compelling reasons to explain the pervasive admiration for the rule of law. Government based on pre-established rules protects the citizenry from governance riding the winds and whims of those wielding power. Justice Benjamin Cardozo denounced governance premised on the will of officials. "That might result in a benevolent despotism," he observed, "if judges," or presidents, for that matter, "were benevolent men." He warned, however, that it "would put an end to the reign of law."[5] And to the values and principles of republicanism, we might add.

Governmental officials, it is familiar, have no authority to deviate from the principles of the Constitution and the rule of law. How could they, after all, when they derive their authority from the Constitution? In 1957, Justice Hugo Black gave expression to the First Principle of American Constitutionalism: "The United States is entirely a creature of the Constitution. Its powers and authority have no other source. It can act only in accordance with all the limitations imposed by the Constitution."[6] The principle that government may exercise only that authority—enumerated or implied—conferred upon it by the Constitution, would insure subordination of the government to the Constitution, the essence of the rule of law. The doctrine of the "consent of the governed" was implemented in 1780 in the Massachusetts Constitution, the world's oldest written Constitution, and four other state constitutions written in the founding years. John Adams, the principal author of the Massachusetts document, declared: "The people

---

[4] For discussion of the Bush Administration's assertions of sweeping executive power, see Adler, "George Bush and the Abuse of History," *UCLA Journal of Int. Affairs* (Spring 2007). (Adler 2007).

[5] Benjamin N. Cardozo, *The Nature of the Judicial Process* (New Haven: Yale University Press, 1921), p. 136. (Cardozo 1921).

[6] *Reid v. Covert*, 354 U.S. 1,16–17 (1957).

have a right to require of their ... magistrates and exact constant observance" of the "fundamental principles of the Constitution."[7] Conformity of the government to the provisions of the Constitution was the *sine qua non* of the doctrine of popular sovereignty. Alexander Hamilton, writing in *Federalist No. 22*, drew attention to the Framers' understanding of the crucial linkage between popular sovereignty and governmental actions: "The fabric of the American empire, ought to rest on the solid basis of THE CONSENT OF THE PEOPLE." James Wilson, second in importance to James Madison as an architect of the Constitution, had earlier championed the principle when he observed that, "The binding power of the law flowed from the continuous assent of the subjects of law."[8]

While the daily implementation of the rule of law may be more a goal than a consistent practice, pursuit of that goal is integral to our national interest. The rule of law promotes limited government, confined within its constitutional allocation of power, protects against arbitrariness, urges official conduct in accord with known rules and procedures, counters assertions of unlimited discretion and power; fulfills the will of the people, as manifested in their ratification of the Constitution, and promotes stability and predictability. In principle and practice, the rule of law means that officials may not undertake actions that are prohibited by the Constitution. As James Madison observed, "[I]t is our duty ... to take care that the powers of the Constitution be preserved entire to every department of Government; the breach of the Constitution in one point, will facilitate the breach in another."[9]

This is all the more important when considering the nature and impact of warfare—the great toll on the blood and treasure of the United States, the sweeping psychological and personal impact on the citizenry, and the potential destruction of government and country. The dutiful declaration by men and women who are on the cusp of taking their countries to war, a

---

[7] Article XVIII, Benjamin P. Poore, ed., *Federal and State Constitutions, Colonial Charters*, 2 vols., I:959; New Hampshire (1784), Article 38, 2 Poore 1283; North Carolina (1776), Article XXI, 2 Poore 1410; Pennsylvania (1776), Article XIV, 2 Poore 1542; Vermont (1777), Article XVI, 2 Poore 1860.

[8] Hamilton, *Federalist No. 22*, p. 141 (Mod. Lib. Ed., 1937) (emphasis in original). Wilson, quoted in Bernard Bailyn, *The Ideological Origins of the American Revolution* (Cambridge, MA, 1967), 174. (Bailyn 1967).

[9] 1 Annals of Congress 500.

soulful apology made in advance of the initiation of hostilities that "the decision to go to war is the most awesome decision that any government could make," was, for the Framers of the Constitution, certainly no cliché. The founding generation had experienced war first hand, and many of the delegates to the Constitutional Convention were veterans of the Revolutionary War and other battles with Native Americans. The decision to go to war, moreover, was grounded in the founders' deep appreciation of history, which was riddled with examples of personal wars among sovereigns, which wagered the lives of subjects for arbitrary reasons and causes. Thus it was that, to a man, the Convention opted to vest the war power—the authority to initiate hostilities on behalf of Americans—in Congress, and not in the president.

The unanimous decision of delegates to the Convention to vest the war power in Congress was a function, principally, of two factors. First, the Founders exhibited a deep distrust of executive power, born of their experience under King George III, whom they resented as a "tyrant," and their keen reading of history, which taught them that executives across the centuries—kings, despots, and tyrants—had marched their people into war for less than meritorious reasons, often to serve their own personal predilections, finances, and political agendas. Second, the Framers were committed to the creation of a republic, which, they believed, was best served by reliance on collective decision making, and not the unilateral determinations of an executive. The Framers' decision to grant the war power to Congress was clear and straightforward. They had confidence that a solemn discussion and debate on the relative merits of going to war would produce a wiser decision than leaving that critical choice to the views and values of a single person. As James Wilson put it, the Framers designed a system to prevent "one man from hurrying us into war." At bottom, then, the Framers broke radically from the "executive model," which concentrated in the executive authority over matters of war and peace.[10]

---

[10] For detailed examination and analysis of the Framers' discussions and debates on the war power, see, generally, Louis Fisher, *Presidential War Power*, 3rd ed. Revised (Lawrence, KS, 2013) (Fisher 2013); Adler, "Constitution and Presidential Warmaking," *Political Science Quarterly* 103, No. 1–36 (1988), 1–36 (Adler 1988), and sources cited in note 94. See, also, Francis D. Wormuth and Edwin B. Firmage, *To Chain the Dog of War: The War Power in History and Law* (Dallas,

The Framers' fear of "one man" taking the nation into war, the concept of unilateral presidential war-making is, in my mind, as sound and real in our time, as it was two centuries ago. The founding generation, experienced as it was with war, and the pain, misery, and costs associated with it, could never have glimpsed the horrors of modern warfare, all of which may be unleashed by a single person—the U.S. president—if unilateral executive war making remains the practice in America, despite the fact that the practice violates the Constitution. But the political and policy debates about the relative merits of unilateral presidential war-making versus congressional decision making on the matter of initiating war, whether by formal declaration or joint resolution authorizing military hostilities, is thus fundamentally a matter of values. Are America's national security interests better served by the decisions of one person or those resulting from group decision-making? The Framers' preference was clear, as reflected in James Wilson's declaration that the Constitution prohibits unilateral executive war making. But the question that drives this book is whether the Constitution remains adequate for the United States in an age of terrorism? The Constitution, it bears reminder, is, by the terms of the Supremacy Clause (Article VI), the "Supreme Law of the Land." Unless, and until, resort is made to the Amendatory Clause of the Constitution—Article V—the War Clause is the only *constitutional* model for commencing war. Arguments for presidential war-making, if they prove persuasive on policy grounds, must appeal on an altogether higher plane: they must persuade the American people to amend the Constitution and vest the war power in the executive. The War on Terror has provided a backdrop for renewed assertions

1986), (Wormuth and Firmage 1986); James P. Pfiffner, *Power Play: The Bush Presidency and the Constitution* (Washington, D.C., 2008); Frederick A. O. Schwarz Jr. and Aziz Z. Huq, *Unchecked and Unbalanced: Presidential Power in a Time of Terror* (New York, 2007). For the view that the president possesses unilateral war-making authority and, indeed, plenary powers in the conduct of American foreign policy, see the works of John Yoo, including *The Powers of War and Peace: The Constitution and Foreign Affairs After 9/11* (Chicago, 2005). For more recent commentary, see Charlie Savage, *Power Wars: Inside Obama's Post-9/11 Presidency* (New York, 2015), and Chris on Terror Edelson, *Emergency Presidential Power: From the Drafting of the Constitution to the War on Terror* (Madison: University of Wisconsin Press, 2013).

of greater executive power in matters of war and peace, but we have yet to hear from advocates of unilateral presidential war making any proposals to initiate a great national debate to amend the War Clause of the Constitution. Such proposals may yet emerge, but regardless of those prospects, review and analysis of arguments on behalf of presidential war making are a matter of urgency, given that their claims assert sweeping executive power to initiate military hostilities.

Rationales for far-reaching executive authority, essentially self-serving claims for untethered presidential power, are demonstrably false. "The refutation of an argument," Chief Justice Thomas McKean declared to the Pennsylvania Ratifying Convention, "begets a proof" and compels consideration of an alternative view—the fact that the Framers created a presidency with sharply limited authority, which did not entail a unilateral war-making power. Misleading accounts of the Framers' discussions and conclusions, especially those surrounding such pivotal matters as war and peace and national security, require a response lest victory, as John Locke wrote in 1689, be "adjudged not to him who had truth on his side, but by the last word in the dispute."[11] For a nation founded on the consent of the governed and committed to the rule of law, a grasp of the constitutional governance of the war power, critical to security and survival, is of surpassing importance. As Arthur Schlesinger, Jr. justly wrote: "If citizens are unwilling to study the processes by which foreign policy is made, they have only themselves to blame when they go marching off to war."[12]

---

[11] McKean, quoted in *Debates in the Several State Conventions on the Adoption of the Federal Convention*, 2nd edition, ed. Jonathan Elliott 2 (Washington, D.C., 1836), p. 251; Locke, *An Essay Concerning Human Understanding* (Oxford, 1894), 242–243. Locke's teachings were instructive for Thomas Jefferson. Alexander Hamilton's constitutional arguments in support of President George Washington's Proclamation of Neutrality infuriated Jefferson, who commissioned James Madison to refute them. "Nobody answers him," he wrote, and "his doctrines will therefore be taken for confessed. For God's Sake, my dear Sir, take up your pen, select the most striking heresies and cut him to pieces in the face of the public." Letter from Jefferson to Madison (July 7, 1793), in *The Writings of Thomas Jefferson 1792–1794*, p. 338.

[12] Schlesinger, *Foreword* to *The Constitution and the Conduct of American Foreign Policy*, eds. Adler and George, p. ix. (Adler and George 1996).

THE CONSTITUTIONAL ARRANGEMENT FOR WAR REMAINS ADEQUATE

Professor Genovese is surely correct in his conclusion that the United States does not need to resort to the institutionalization of an Imperial Presidency on matters of war and peace in order to maintain our national security. He could not be more right about that; indeed, for the past three decades I have criticized the unbridled assertions of executive power in the realm of foreign affairs.[13] I disagree, however, with his desire to "bolster the presidency" in the age of terrorism. In fact, it is not clear, given the steady practice of unilateral executive war making—and presidential usurpation of foreign affairs authority—over the past sixty years, exactly which additional powers might be further aggrandized by a White House already exerting plenary powers in the realm of national security. In the aftermath of September 11, 2001, President George W. Bush, in his capacity as wartime executive, advanced the theory of a "Unitary Presidency" to assert under the banner of inherent presidential power and the Commander in Chief Clause a scope of authority so sweeping that it traduced the doctrines of separation of powers and checks and balances. The president, according to the Bush Administration's legal theory of presidential power in foreign affairs, might initiate preventive war, without authorization

---

[13] See, generally, Adler, "The Framers and Treaty Termination: A Matter of Symmetry," *Arizona State Law Journal* (1981), pp. 891–923; Adler, "The Constitution and Presidential War-Making: The Enduring Debate," *Political Science Quarterly* 103 (1988), 1–36 (Adler 1988); Adler, "The President's Recognition Power," in *The Constitution and the Conduct of American Foreign Policy*, eds. Adler and Larry N. George (University Press of Kansas, 1995), pp. 133–158 (Adler and George 1996); Louis Fisher and David Gray Adler, "The War Powers Resolution: Time to Say Goodbye," *Political Science Quarterly* 113 (1988), 1–20 (1998) (Fisher and Adler 1998); Adler, "The Clinton Theory of the War Power," *Presidential Studies Quarterly* 30 (March 2000), 155–169; Adler, "Virtues of the War Clause," *Presidential Studies Quarterly* 30 (December 2000), 777–783; Adler, "George Bush and the Abuse of History: The Constitution and Presidential Power in Foreign Affairs," *UCLA Journal of International Law and Foreign Affairs* 12 (Spring 2007), 75–144 (Adler 2007); Adler, "Presidential Power and Foreign Affairs: The Use and Abuse of Alexander Hamilton," *Presidential Studies Quarterly* 40 (September 2010), 531–545.

from Congress. As commander in chief, he possesses the sole and exclusive authority to conduct war. Congressional directions and instructions are invidious, constitute micromanagement, and represent an encroachment on presidential power. The president may institute domestic surveillance of Americans' telephone calls and e-mails as part and parcel of his authority to wage war on terrorism. Statutes in conflict with the president's policies represent a violation of executive authority. The administration contended that the president may designate, seize and detain any American citizen as an "enemy combatant" and imprison him in solitary confinement, indefinitely, without access to legal counsel and a judicial hearing. The Constitution, it was asserted, provided no right of habeas corpus to American citizens. It was maintained, moreover, that the president possessed the authority to suspend the Geneva Convention and the federal laws that prohibit torture. Among other powers asserted, the president, as commander in chief, may establish military tribunals, terminate treaties, orders acts of extraordinary rendition, and take actions that he perceived necessary to the maintenance of national security and the common defense. Under this theory, any law that restricts the authority of the commander in chief is presumptively unconstitutional. At all events, the president may exercise an "over-ride" authority in the unlikely event that Congress would by statute seek to restrain the president. Courts have no role to play in matters of war and peace, but if they do entertain lawsuits, they should defer to the president and refrain from second-guessing his foreign policy.

President Bush's theory of the scope of his authority is a reminder of what Gerhard Casper described as the most dangerous and pervasive of all constitutional myths—the myth that in foreign affairs, "the president is Zeus."[14] Like this greatest of Olympian gods, whose power was supreme and whose behavior was beyond control, the president, according to this myth, may do whatever he wishes in the realm of American foreign affairs. This far-reaching, virtually unrestrained conception of executive power finds no footing in the provisions of the Constitution or the principles of republicanism.

[14] Gerhard Casper, "Constitutional Constraints on the Conduct of Foreign Policy: A Nonjudicial Model," *Chicago Law Review* 43 (1976), 477; reprinted in Adler and George, eds., *Constitution and the Conduct of American Foreign Policy*, 259–274. (Adler and George 1996).

Professor Genovese and I agree on several key points. For example, it is clear to both of us that Congress is vested with the sole and exclusive authority to initiate military hostilities. We further agree, much to our frustration and disappointment, that while Congress possesses the necessary constitutional power to commence war, that it has been utterly spineless in performing its responsibilities in the realm of national security. As a consequence, presidential usurpation of the war power has been matched, so it would seem, by congressional abdication and acquiescence. Our mutual frustration leads us, moreover, to agreement that the Constitution should be amended to prohibit the President from engaging in "unauthorized" war making which, indeed, should be made an impeachable offense. I confess to concluding, however, that that wish is unlikely to be fulfilled without a resurgent Congress, triggered, perhaps, by a citizenry exhausted by governmental indifference to the Constitution. We happily find additional agreement on the virtues of retroactive ratification of presidential acts that were, when committed, illegal and perhaps unconstitutional. Emergencies are bound to occur, and if they do and if the president meets the challenge of the emergency, in the absence of law or in defiance of it, he must seek retroactive authorization from Congress. Genovese would have the president seek it, in some fashion, from Congress, the courts or the public. I contend that only Congress may provide such authorization, and have embraced it in scholarly writings stretching across three decades.[15]

Professor Genovese and I differ in important respects. As indicated, I take issue with his assertion that "we may need to bolster the presidency" on grounds that the president can move quickly, a prerequisite of the demands imposed by the "War on Terror." This argument about the need for "speed and dispatch," it seems to me, is overvalued and fraught with peril. If the United States is attacked then, of course, we need to act as quickly as possible, but the Constitution vests that responsibility in the

---

[15] See, e.g., David Gray Adler, "The Constitution and Presidential War-Making: The Enduring Debate," *Political Science Quarterly* 103 (Spring 1988), 1–36 (Adler 1988); Adler, "Constitution, Foreign Affairs and Presidential War-Making: A Response to Professor Powell," *Georgia State University Law Review* 19 (Summer 2003), 947–1019 (Adler 2003b); Adler, "George Bush and the Abuse of History," *UCLA Journal of Int. Law and Foreign Affairs*, 114–120. (Adler 2007).

president, in his capacity as commander in chief, to "repel the invasion." But there is a world of difference between reliance on the president to respond to an attack on America, on the order of Pearl Harbor and 9/11, and empowering the president to initiate military hostilities abroad. "Presidential wars" in Korea and Vietnam, as well as the flawed and misleading reports that paved the way for the invasion of Iraq in 2003, illuminate some of the problems surrounding unilateral presidential war-making. In my view, Professor Genovese overestimates the quality and reliability of presidential decision-making. Of course, much the same criticism may be leveled at Congress, which is unwilling to shoulder its constitutional responsibilities in war and foreign affairs. Still, there is enduring merit in the concept of deliberation, discussion, and debate—the hallmarks of a vigorous Congress—in foreign policy and national security, if only the lawmakers will engage it. A denial of the value of deliberations and debates would represent a denial of republicanism itself.

We disagree, manifestly, on the need to reform the constitutional process for going to war. Professor Genovese contends that the Constitution is "ill-suited to the needs of the twenty-first century," while I maintain that it is fully adequate for making the decision to go to war. His proposal for the "Gang of Eight" to play an authoritative role in decisions about war making has merit in advocating greater executive-legislative "consultation," but falls short, in my view, in explaining how to "require" the president to consult with Congress. The War Powers Act of 1973 includes a consultation requirement, but there has been little willingness on the part of presidents to abide by it and little interest in congressional enforcement of it. There remains the problem, as he acknowledges, of infusing Congress with the backbone to perform its constitutional duties on matters of war and peace.[16]

My approach to the problem that we address in this book—whether the Constitution is adequate to the war-making and national security needs of the United States in an age of terror—is two-fold. First, we examine the arguments and claims made on behalf of unilateral presidential war making. Second, we seek to persuade readers that the constitutional design for war and peace is not obsolescent but, indeed,

---

[16] For analysis of the War Powers Act, see Fisher and Adler, "The War Powers Resolution: Time to Say Goodbye."

as compelling today, if not more so, than it was in 1787, when the Framers of the Constitution drafted both the War Clause and the Commander-in-Chief Clause.

If advocates for greater presidential power than that conferred by the Constitution should prove successful in their cause, it bears reminder that their work toward that goal must cross a critical threshold: passage of a constitutional amendment. The mere desire for an additional power does not create it. As James Madison said of the treaty power, "Had the power of making treaties, for example, been omitted, however necessary it might have been, the defect could only have been lamented, or supplied by an amendment of the Constitution."[17] In 1803, in *Marbury* v. *Madison*, it will be recalled, Chief Justice Marshall struck down, in the first exercise of the power of judicial review in the Court's history, a section of a statute that would have increased the scope of the Court's constitutionally granted "judicial power," which it derives from Article III.[18]

To date, there has been no serious or sustained effort by advocates of a unilateral presidential war power to engage the nation in a grand amendatory dialogue on the purported merits of abolishing the constitutional design for foreign affairs and national security. Their quarrel, frankly, is with the Framers of the Constitution, who sharply rejected unilateral executive power on matters of war and peace, and with the American people, who have evinced no perceptible interest in amending the Constitution for the purpose of transferring the war power to the president. There is, in their critiques and criticisms of the grant of war-making authority to Congress, rather than the president, no call to arms for an amendatory effort; indeed, there is no mention of the availability of Article V as a remedy for what they perceive as the obsolescence of the War Clause. Nor have they proffered a constitutional theory that would legitimate presidential usurpation of the war power. Rather, they have sought justification for presidential aggrandizement in three policy arguments: (1) the doctrine of changing circumstances, (2) superior executive information, and (3) congressional incoherence. But policy preferences cannot overcome constitutional principles. As Chief Justice Marshall wrote in his defense of *McCulloch* v. *Maryland* (1819): "The

---

[17] Annals of Congress, I: 503 (1789).
[18] 5 U.S. [I Cranch] 137 (1803).

peculiar circumstances of the moment may render a measure more or less wise, but cannot render it more or less constitutional."[19]

We shall review and examine the planks and pillars of the platform of unilateral presidential war making, for the purpose of demonstrating that they cannot withstand scrutiny: the commander in chief and Vesting Clauses of Article II of the Constitution; claims of inherent executive power; assertions of historical precedent; and, among others, the contention that, as the "sole organ" of American foreign policy, the president enjoys plenary authority in the realm of matters of national security. In addition, we will analyze policy arguments made on behalf of presidential war-making to show that the claims of superior information, experience, and expertise of the president in issues involving war and peace, as well as the argument for speed and dispatch in the age of terrorism are unpersuasive. In addition, we will review the assertion that courts have no role to play in matters of war and peace, but if they do entertain lawsuits, they should defer to the president and refrain from second-guessing his acts. Finally, we will lay bare the poverty of the claim that Congress should not enact statutes that conflict with presidential authority to make decisions on the initiation of military hostilities, large or small.

HISTORICAL BACKGROUND ON THE CONSTITUTION AND NATIONAL SECURITY

Few issues in the life of a nation rival in importance the maintenance of national security, the conduct of foreign policy, and decisions on matters of war and peace. The premise is as true today as it was for the Framers of the Constitution, for whom the search for an efficient foreign policy design was a primary and animating purpose of the Constitutional Convention. Alexander Hamilton, for example, lamented the chaos in American foreign policy inspired by the disparate views and policy interests of the states under the Articles of Confederation: "The faith, the reputation, the peace of the whole union, are thus continually at the mercy of the prejudices, the passions, and the interests of every member of which these are composed. Is it possible that foreign nations can either respect or

---

[19] Quoted in Gerald Gunther, *John Marshall's Defense of McCulloch v. Maryland* (Palo Alto: Stanford University Press, 1969), 190–191. (Gunther 1969).

confide in such a government?"[20] Such was the concern about foreign policy that nearly all of the first thirty *Federalist Papers* addressed some facet of national security. The Articles of Confederation attributed to Congress no effective authority to enforce treaties, raise revenues, create armies, or wage war. The deficiencies moved Hamilton to complain: "We have neither troops, nor treasury, nor government."[21]

The Framers, it is familiar, rejected the English Model—the monarchical model, a design that emphasized executive unilateralism—for the conduct of foreign affairs. The concept of unilateral executive control of foreign policy was, for the Founders, intolerable, and never was within their sights. In their view, the executive model was obsolete; it belonged to an earlier age, the world of monarchy, one ill-suited to the new age of republicanism aborning in America. As a consequence, their constitutional design for foreign affairs and national security embodied the principle of collective decision making— shared powers, discussion, debate, and checks and balances—in the formulation, management and oversight of American foreign policy.[22]

---

[20] *The Federalist No. 22*, (George W. Carey & James McClellan, eds. 2001), 111.

[21] The *Federalist No. 15*, 69.

[22] In the Constitutional Convention, James Wilson, second in importance to James Madison as an architect of the Constitution, and a future Supreme Court Justice, declared that "the prerogatives of the British Crown [are not] a proper guide in defining the Executive powers." *The Records of the Federal Convention of 1787, 1* (M. Farrand ed., 1911), pp. 65–66. In order to allay fears that the Convention had created an embryonic monarch, Hamilton launched into a minute analysis of presidential power in *Federalist No. 71* and noted that nothing "was to be feared" from an executive "with the confined authorities of a president of the United States." *The Federalist No. 71*, p. 373.

In the First Congress, Roger Sherman, who had been a delegate at the Convention, argued in defense of the shared-power arrangement in foreign affairs: "The more wisdom there is employed, the greater security there is that the public business will be done." I Annals of Congress 1123 (Joseph Gales ed., 1834) (1790). The Framers' attachment to collective decision making in foreign affairs reflected, in part, their distrust of executive unilateralism. Hamilton explained that the treaty power—the essential vehicle for formulating foreign policy in the minds of the Framers—was withheld from the president since it was not "wise" to commit such awesome authority to a single individual. Greater wisdom and security would be procured by combining the skills and strengths of the president and the Senate in treaty-making. *The Federalist No. 75*, 389.

Yet no feature of recent governmental practice has more vexed, betrayed, and disfigured the Constitution than executive aggrandizement of war and foreign affairs powers. Until 1950, it had been long established and well settled that the Constitution vests in Congress the sole and exclusive authority to initiate total as well as limited war. But since then, that firm understanding has been subjected to a continuing assault by advocates of unilateral executive war-making powers. Harry S. Truman was the first president to claim constitutional authority to initiate war when he deployed American troops to Korea and plunged the United States into a bloody and intractable civil war. The Truman Administration and its advocates laid claim to broad executive powers to justify the president's unprecedented assertions. Emboldened by Truman's assertions, subsequent presidents, including, most recently, George W. Bush and Barack Obama, have likewise unilaterally initiated war, often with the acquiescence of Congress. These executive assertions, which have established a consistent pattern of aggrandizement and usurpation, have been grounded on, among other claims, the alleged authority that the president derives from the Vesting Clause, the Commander-in-Chief Clause and the "sole organ" doctrine. These contentions threaten to eviscerate the War Clause of the Constitution, which vests the war power solely and exclusively in Congress, not the president.

An accurate recovery of the work of the Constitutional Convention assumes vital importance when judges, presidents and commentators draw upon the debates in Philadelphia to adduce constitutional meaning. "Legal history," Justice Felix Frankfurter wrote, "still has its claims." Constitutional interpretation is, indeed, rooted in history. Historical pitfalls and errors aside, the Supreme Court's regard for the aims and intentions of the Framers of the Constitution remain high. The distinguished constitutional scholar, Alexander Bickel, rejected "the proposition that the original understanding is simply not relevant. For arguments based on that understanding...have been relied on by judges well aware that it is a *constitution* they were expounding."[23]

---

[23] Frankfurter, concurring opinion, in Fed. Power Comm'n v. Natural Gas Pipeline Co. of America, 315 U.S. 575, 609. Bickel, "The Original Understanding and the Segregation Decision," *Harvard Law Review* 69 (1955), 1, 3–4 (emphasis in original). (Bickel 1955).

Invocations of the original understanding of the Constitution were renewed by the Bush Administration in the aftermath of 9/11 in an effort to advance a capacious view of presidential power. The assertions of the meaning of the War Clause, the Vesting Clause and the Commander in Chief Clause, reflected earlier renditions produced by presidents of both parties, Republicans and Democrats, conservatives and liberals alike, as seen in the advocacy of the administrations of Lyndon Johnson, Richard Nixon, Ronald Reagan, Bill Clinton, and George H. W. Bush. The Administration of Barack Obama has, in important ways, followed suit. These chief executives claimed that the president, as commander in chief, possesses the unilateral authority to initiate military hostilities on behalf of the American people. The Bush Administration's assertion of the president's sweeping powers to use military force was set forth two weeks after September 11, 2001, in a memorandum written by John Yoo, an attorney in the Office of Legal Counsel. He concluded that "the Constitution vests the President with the plenary authority, as commander in chief and sole organ of the nation in its foreign relations, to use military force abroad—especially in response to grave national emergencies created by sudden, unforeseen attacks on the people and territory of the United States."[24] Yoo had earlier written that, on the basis of English history, "the Framers created a framework designed to encourage presidential initiative in war. Congress was given a role in war-making decisions not by the Declare War Clause, but by its powers over funding and impeachment."[25] In addition, federal courts were to have no role at all. The Yoo Memorandum gave voice to the Bush Administration's view that the Framers provided for presidential domination of war and foreign affairs. Let us consider that contention.

Professor Jefferson Powell provided a similar view of presidential power in foreign affairs in his book, *The President's Authority over Foreign Affairs: An Essay in Constitutional Interpretation*, published in 2002. There, Professor Powell offered his "best" reading of the "Constitution

---

[24] Memorandum Opinion from John C. Yoo, Deputy Assistant Attorney General, for the Deputy Counsel to the president (September 25, 2001) (regarding The President's Constitutional Authority to Conduct Military Operations against Terrorists and Nations Supporting Them).

[25] Yoo, "Judicial Review and the War on Terrorism," *George Washington Law Review* 72 (2003), 427. (Yoo 2003).

of foreign affairs," a view that promotes presidential domination, which he characterizes as "the President's legally-unbounded authority over United States foreign policy."[26] His thesis, which exalts the concept of executive ascendancy, is not far removed from that of Justice George Sutherland, who asserted in 1936, in *United States v. Curtiss-Wright Export Corporation*, that the President is the "sole organ" of American foreign policy. While it is clear that neither the Sutherland opinion nor its scholarly progeny can find comfort in the Constitution, it has been true for roughly eighty years that the president has been functioning as the sole organ of U.S. foreign relations, largely unchallenged by a quiescent legislature and unchecked by a deferential judiciary. For the record, Professor Powell argues that "the reality of current practice is not too distant from what it should be in principle."[27]

THE CLAIM: PLENARY EXECUTIVE FOREIGN AFFAIRS POWERS

The assertion of a plenary presidential power over foreign affairs finds no support in the text of the Constitution, debates in the Constitutional Convention, the *Federalist Papers* or early Supreme Court precedents. In fact, the very concept of plenary executive authority in foreign relations was rejected in the Convention. The Framers might have embraced the executive—or English—model for reasons of familiarity, tradition, and simplicity, as a means of promoting and securing its vaunted values of unity, secrecy, and dispatch—but they did not. The Framers were thoroughly familiar with both the vast foreign affairs powers that inhered in the English Crown by virtue of the royal prerogative, and the values, sentiments, and policy concerns that justified this arrangement. In his *Second Treatise of Government*, John Locke described three powers of government: legislative, executive, and federative. The federative power, Locke explained, entailed authority over foreign affairs powers. It was, he wrote, "almost always united" with the executive. He warned that the separation of executive and federative powers would invite "disorder and ruin."[28] Sir William

---

[26] Powell, *The President's Authority Over Foreign Affairs: An Essay in Constitutional Interpretation* (Durham: Carolina Academic Press, 2002), 122. (Powell 2002).

[27] 299 U.S. 304 (1936); Powell, *President's Authority*, p. xv (Powell 2002).

[28] John Locke, *The Second Treatise of Government*, secs. 146–148 (1690).

Blackstone, the great eighteenth-century jurist, explained his magisterial four-volume Commentaries on the Law of England, that the king possessed plenary authority over all matters relating to war and peace, diplomacy, treaties, and military command. The king's prerogative, Blackstone wrote, "is, and ought to be absolute; that is, so far absolute that there is no legal authority that can either delay or resist him."[29]

The Convention's rejection of the English model could not have been more emphatic. The constitutional design for foreign affairs reflects the Framers' commitment to the establishment of a republic which, of course, is grounded on collective decision making, a principle that reflects confidence in the crossfire of discussion and debate for generating superior laws, policies, and programs. Their belief in the value of deliberation and debate provided the cornerstone for the construction of the republic, a belief manifested in the design for foreign affairs and, later, in the guarantee in the First Amendment of freedom of speech. The republic, it should be recalled, is a system of government built on values that course through the Constitution.

The preference for collective, rather than unilateral, decision making runs throughout the constitutional provisions that govern American foreign policy. The Constitution assigns to Congress senior status in a partnership with the president for the purpose of formulating, managing and conducting the nation's foreign affairs. A series of discrete powers, granted to both Congress and the president, illuminate the Framers' decision to fragment authority over foreign affairs, a clear disregard for Locke's warning that shared powers would result in disaster and ruin. Article I vests in Congress broad, explicit, and exclusive powers to regulate foreign commerce, raise and maintain military forces, grant letters of marque and reprisal, provide for the common defense, and initiate hostilities on behalf of the United States, including full-blown war. As Article II indicates, the president shares with the Senate the treaty making power and the authority to appoint ambassadors. The Constitution exclusively assigns two foreign affairs powers to the president. He is designated commander in chief of the nation's armed forces although, as we shall see, he acts in this capacity by and under the authority of Congress. The president also has the duty to receive ambassadors, but the Framers viewed

---

[29] William Blackstone, *Commentaries on the Laws of England*, 2 (1765–1769), 238–250. (Blackstone 1765–1769).

this as a routine, administrative function, devoid of discretionary authority. This list exhausts the textual grant of authority to Congress and the president. The president's powers are few and modest, and they pale in comparison to those vested in Congress. The American arrangement bears no resemblance to the English model. The assertion of a plenary presidential power over foreign affairs is utterly without foundation.

Behind the Framers' emphatic rejection of the British model, grounded in a strong distrust of unilateral executive authority, lay an equally emphatic commitment to the republican principle of collective decision-making—the belief that the conjoined wisdom of the many is superior to that of one. The Framers perceived a broad equatorial divide between the hemispheres of monarchism and republicanism, and the values of the Old World and the New World. The Framers' deliberate fragmentation of powers relating to diplomacy, treaties, and war and peace, the allocation of various foreign affairs powers to different departments and agencies of government, shed light on their decision to apply the doctrines of separation of powers and checks and balances, the principle of the rule of law, and the elements of constitutionalism to the realm of foreign relations as rigorously as they had been applied to the domestic domain.

A historian gazing upon this chain of events, this upheaval of conventional wisdom regarding the allocation of foreign affairs powers, would conclude that the Framers regarded unification and centralization of foreign affairs powers as obsolete and ill-suited to the needs of a republic. Accordingly, those in our time who urge concentration of foreign relations powers in the executive would surrender the views, values and wisdom of the Framers' to embrace the British monarchical trappings that the founders rejected.

THE CLAIM: UNILATERAL PRESIDENTIAL POWER TO USE FORCE

Presidents Bush and Obama, like their predecessors dating back to Harry Truman, have invoked the Commander-in-Chief Clause as authority to wage war on behalf of the United States. The claim of unilateral presidential power to initiate military hostilities, including the authority to wage war, finds no support in the text of the Constitution, the debates in Philadelphia and various state ratifying conventions, the *Federalist Papers* and other writings contemporaneous to the drafting of the Constitution, or in early Supreme Court decisions. In short, the claim finds no support in our constitutional architecture.

On October 9, 2001, President Bush sent a letter to congressional leaders on military actions in Afghanistan. He explained that he had ordered the acts "pursuant to my constitutional authority to conduct U.S. foreign relations as Commander in Chief and Chief Executive."[30] Moreover, after signing the Iraq Resolution passed by Congress on October 20, 2002, a measure which purported to authorize military action against Iraq, President Bush acknowledged the legislation as a "resolution of support," but added that his act of signing the resolution did not "constitute any change in the long standing position of the executive branch on either the President's constitutional authority to use force to deter, prevent, or respond to aggression or other threats to U.S. interests or on the constitutionality of the War Powers Resolution."[31] While Bush echoed the constitutional arguments of some of his recent predecessors, he soared to new heights with his claim in the National Security Strategy of presidential authority to initiate preventive war.[32] Bush's assertion of unilateral presidential authority to strike other nations on the premise that they might, someday, somehow, strike the United States, represented an unprecedented assertion of authority to launch preventive strikes. Bush's claims are wholly without merit and wildly at odds with the constitutional design for matters of war and peace. They are, moreover, sheer folly. The assertion of a unilateral executive power to initiate preventive war, grounded on the President's perception of a gathering threat, is but a poor rival to the claim of papal infallibility, and invites scorn and ridicule if, for no other reason, than that it is a model of governance unworthy of admiration or imitation.

The Framers' rejection of the British model for foreign affairs was nowhere more conspicuous than in their decision to vest the war power in Congress. That decision reflected their overall view that Congress, not the president, should be the principal organ of American foreign policy, and in this conclusion they ignored the dire predictions and warnings of

[30] *Weekly Compilation of Presidential Documents*, 37 (October 15, 2001), 1447.

[31] *Weekly Compilation of Presidential Documents*, 38 (October 21, 2002), 1779.

[32] George Bush, Introduction to the White House, The National Security Strategy of the United States of America (September 17, 2002).

chaos and disaster that would accompany a shared division of the war and foreign affairs powers. At all events, the war power is not an "inherent" executive power. Rather, it is textually enumerated and, therefore, emphatically constitutional.

THE WAR CLAUSE AND THE COMMANDER-IN-CHIEF CLAUSE IN CONTEXT

It is altogether true that for the past sixty years, successive presidents have engaged in unilateral acts of war making without congressional authorization, and it is equally true that on those occasions, Congress took little or no action to preserve its powers from naked usurpation by the executive branch. The list of what Francis D. Wormuth aptly characterized as "presidential wars," is long, from Truman in Korea, to Nixon and Johnson in Vietnam, to Reagan in Grenada, to Bush I in Panama, to Clinton in Iraq and Bosnia, to Bush II in Iraq, to Obama in Libya.

Unilateral executive war making has eroded the War Clause, a landmark constitutional provision, through the introduction of arbitrary power, an act that the Framers sought to preclude by means of a written Constitution that limited governmental authority by assigning specific responsibilities to each branch, dividing authority, and imposing restraints on power. Viewed in the context of history, these acts are in a category with President Truman's assertion of an inherent power to seize the steel mills and President Nixon's claim of an absolute executive privilege. History demonstrates that parchment alone is no match for an executive who has determined to exert power that has not been granted. The War Clause has been all but buried by an avalanche of executive branch missives asserting a unilateral presidential war power.

The justifications for executive war making shatter upon analysis. More than occasionally, presidents have engaged in acts of war without bothering to adduce a constitutional rationale, thus ignoring the duty of all three branches of government to trace their actions, however circuitously, to constitutional norms, as a means of maintaining the rule of law. When they have troubled to supply justification, the strategy, if not the reasoning, has been clear and it has been punctuated with obfuscation. Executive branch attorneys have contended, moreover, that the Constitution is vague and ambiguous in its textual assignment of the repository of authority to initiate hostilities and to decide for war. Across the decades, the terms and tones of presidential assertions of power have been strikingly reminiscent of the imperial chords struck by English kings.

While it may be difficult to ascertain the intentions that lay behind the Framers' crafting of some provisions of the Constitution, there is nothing obscure about their intentions to vest the war power in Congress. In fact, the war power was specifically withheld from the President; he was given only the authority to repel sudden attacks. Only one delegate—Pierce Butler of South Carolina—advanced the notion of a presidential power to initiate war. On August 17, he asserted that the president should possess the war power because he would not initiate hostilities unless the national interest required it. His view was quickly and soundly condemned by delegates who were surprised to hear anyone suggest the idea of an executive war-making power in a republic. The war power, the Framers knew from contemporary treatises on the law of nations, was regarded as a *legislative*, not an *executive*, power.

Give Butler credit, however, for being a quick study. He immediately retreated from his initial position and, by the end of the day, embraced the wisdom of his colleagues on the repository of the war power. In fact, he proposed a motion "to give the Legislature power of peace, as they were to have that of war." The motion, which represented a volte-face on Butler's part, drew no discussion, and it failed on a vote of 10–0. In all likelihood, it was viewed by delegates as utterly superfluous given the understanding that the war power encompassed authority to determine both war and peace.[33] Butler's experience was an embarrassing one for him. In the South Carolina State Ratifying Convention, several months later, he provided his fellow delegates with a report of the discussions and debates at the Constitutional Convention. Among other things, he shared the story of a single Framer in Philadelphia who had had the temerity to suggest the placement of the war power in the hands of the executive. That "fellow," he explained, was overwhelmed by opposition to his motion. Butler did not tell his colleagues in South Carolina that he was that "fellow."

While there are other evidentiary grounds to reject the claim of a unilateral presidential war-making power, the absence of advocacy of the proposition is compelling. The argument for such an executive power *might* be asserted *if* there were some evidence to support it. But with the exception of Pierce Butler's brief flirtation with the concept, no other

[33] Max Farrand, ed., *The Records of the Federal convention of 1787*, 2 (1911), 319.

delegate, at no other point in the Convention, ever promoted it. Delegates to the Convention were united in their decision to grant the war power to Congress.

The Framers' commitment to collective decision making on matters of war and peace was driven, in large measure, by their fear of unilateral executive war making. Their historic decision to reconfigure the role of the executive in foreign affairs, to strip him of important prerogatives that were, at that juncture, universally admired and practiced, thus replaced absolutist pretensions with congressional supremacy and erased the specter of a president swollen with power who might march the citizenry into war for less than meritorious reasons. It was Madison who brought into sharp relief the great concern about unilateral presidential war-making. In a letter to Jefferson, he observed: "The constitution supposes, what the History of all Governments demonstrates, that the Executive is the branch of power most interested in war, and most prone to it. It has accordingly with studied care vested the question of war in the Legislature."[34]

Experience, so often a valuable guide to Convention delegates in their creation of the Constitution, provided important lessons about unilateral executive war-making across the centuries. The Framers understood the desire of executives to achieve fame, glory, greatness, and immortality through the battlefield.[35] In *Federalist No. 4,* John Jay warned that "absolute monarchs will often make war when their nations are to get nothing by it, but for purposes and objects merely personal, such as, a thirst for military glory, revenge for personal affronts, ambition, or private compacts to aggrandize or support their particular families, or partisans." Jay drew the essence of the lesson for American readers: "These, and a variety of other motives, which affect only the mind of the sovereign, often lead him to engage in wars not sanctioned by justice, or the voice and interests of his people."[36]

The distrust of executive power, which colored the Framers' deliberations on the creation of the presidency, punctuated discussions about the war power. In 1793, Madison characterized war as "the true nurse of

---

[34] Letter of Madison to Jefferson, April 2, 1798, in *The Writings of James Madison,* ed. Gaillard Hunt 6 (New York, 1906), 312.

[35] For discussion, see my article, "Presidential Greatness as an Attribute of Warmaking," *Presidential Studies Quarterly* 33 (2003), 466. (Adler 2003a).

[36] John Jay, *Federalist No. 4,* J.R. Pole, ed. (Indianapolis, 2005), 36.

executive aggrandizement . . . In war, the honours [*sic*] and emoluments of office are to be multiplied; and it is the executive patronage under which they are to be enjoyed. It is in war, finally, that laurels are to be gathered; and it is the executive brow they are to encircle. The strongest passions and most dangerous weaknesses of the human breast; ambition, avarice, vanity, the honourable [*sic*] or venial love of fame, are all in conspiracy against the desire and duty of peace."[37]

Madison was on sure footing in drawing these observations about executive war-making across the centuries. While he had been a keen student of history in his collegiate days at The College of New Jersey (now Princeton University), he stepped up his readings in works on the practice and theory of government in the ancient days of Rome and Greece in his preparation of a draft for a new constitution in the winter and spring of 1787. He was familiar with the fact that storied executive leaders—Julius Caesar and Alexander the Great, among many others—had sought to burnish their image, heighten their stature, garner fame and glory, and secure wealth and legacy through the use of military force. Madison and his fellow founders, committed students of history, understood the potentially corruptive, malignant and pernicious effects of the intoxication of power and fever of ambition. Thus it was that Madison could warn that, among the passions of men, from the beginning, or so it seemed, included dreams of military glory, for it represented a crowning achievement. George Logan, a well-known Quaker, echoed the sentiments of the founding generation when he observed in the 1798 that, "wars created by ambitious executives have been undertaken more for their own aggrandizement and power than for the protection of their country."[38]

While the Framers hoped that future presidents would exhibit the virtues and values of republicanism, they were, nevertheless, wary of the temptations of power and the seductions of fame and glory. Fearful that the nation's chief executive might plunge the citizenry into battle for reasons having little to do with merit or the national interest but on other, less virtuous grounds—personal agendas, political motives, and the lure of fortune, among them—the Framers granted to Congress the sole and

---

[37] Madison, "Letters of Helvidius, No. IV" (1793), reprinted in *Madison Writings* 6 (1790–1802), 174.

[38] Quoted in Alexander DeConde, *Presidential Machismo* (Boston, Northeastern University Press, 2000), 18. (DeConde 2000).

exclusive authority to initiate military hostilities, great or small, on behalf of the American people. Founding documents and material lay bare the Framers' concerns about unilateral presidential power, not only in matters of war and peace, but in the conduct of foreign affairs as well. Consider the voice of Alexander Hamilton, in *Federalist No. 75*, where he explained why the Convention *withheld* from the president unilateral authority over the nation's foreign relations: "The history of human virtue does not warrant that exalted opinion of human nature which would make it wise in a nation to commit interests of so delicate and momentous a kind, as those which concern its intercourse with the rest of the world, to the sole disposal of a magistrate created and circumstanced as would be a president of the United States."[39] It was in order to allay fears that the Convention had created an embryonic monarchy that Hamilton launched into a minute analysis of presidential power in *Federalist No. 69*. He concluded that nothing was "to be feared" from an executive "with the confined authorities of the President."[40] No less a personage than George Washington affirmed Hamilton's observation: "The powers of the Executive of the U. States are more definite, and better understood perhaps than those of almost any other country."[41] This theme of the president's "confined authorities," reflected in Madison's proposal at the Convention that executive power should be "confined and defined," and noted in his essay in *Federalist No. 45* that foreign affairs powers are "enumerated," represented the Framers' transparency in efforts to cabin presidential power, a constitutional configuration which we shall explore in a section below, entitled, "The Claim: The Vesting Clause Empowers the President to Initiate War."

The Founders' fears of executive war making, premised on self-serving, rather than national interests, loomed large. An executive with "spirit and ambition," John Adams wrote, "looks forward with satisfaction to the prospect of foreign war, " or other "wished-for-occasions presenting themselves, in which he may draw upon himself the attention and admiration of mankind."[42] Hamilton, no stranger to intrigue himself, wrote in *The Federalist No. 6*, that some wars "take their wars in private passions,"

---

[39] Alexander Hamilton, *Federalist No. 75*, 487.

[40] Alexander Hamilton, *Federalist No. 69*, 448.

[41] Quoted in Deconde, 16. (DeConde 2000)

[42] *Works of John Adams* 6 (1969), 260.

and that leaders "have in too many instances abused the confidence they possessed; and assuming the pretext of public motive, have not scrupled to sacrifice the national tranquility to personal advantage, or personal gratification."[43] At bottom, the passions, ambition and thirst for glory, rendered the president, in the view of the Framers, unfit to initiate military hostilities. Concerns, moreover, about foreign efforts to "bribe" the president peppered discussions in Philadelphia, particularly when debate moved to the allocation of foreign affairs powers, including the treaty power. Rejection of unilateral executive powers in foreign affairs reflected delegates' reasoning that it was easier to bribe a single person, rather than a group of men. Where the president was assigned a unilateral role in foreign affairs, it tended toward a "ceremonial duty," as seen in the president's "duty" under the Reception Clause to receive foreign ambassadors and ministers.[44] The president's role as commander in chief, as we shall see, was subordinate to the authority of Congress to issue directions and instructions, marking outer boundaries in the use of military force. Checks and balances on executive authority were implemented to relieve anxiety about presidential power. Consider, finally, that the president's "pardon power," which raised concerns of abuse among delegates to the Convention, was made more palatable by the availability of impeachment for the abuse of power, as well as the fact, explained by Hamilton in *Federalist No. 74*, that "the eyes of the nation" would be upon the President in his exercise of the pardon authority, a check that the Framers regarded as a sufficient restraint.[45]

The Framers' assumption that history demonstrated an abiding belief that an executive's road to greatness ran through the battlefield shaped their design of the war power. Indeed, their grant of war-making authority to Congress represented a thoroughly republican response to executive

---

[43] Alexander Hamilton, *Federalist No. 6*, 28.

[44] Adler, "The President's Recognition Power," in *The Constitution and the Conduct of American Foreign Policy*, eds. Adler and George, 133–158 (Adler and George 1996); Adler, "Jerusalem Passport Case: Judicial Error and the Expansion of the President's Recognition Power," *Presidential Studies Quarterly* 44 (Summer 2014), 537–554. (Adler 2014).

[45] Adler, "The President's Pardon Power," in *Inventing the American Presidency*, ed. Thomas E. Cronin (Lawrence, KS: University Press of Kansas, 1989), 209–235. (Cronin 1989).

war making. Madison praised the decision of delegates to the Convention for the wisdom that they exhibited in their decision that "confides the question of war or peace to the legislature, and not to the executive department."[46] Delegates recognized that executive war making was an invitation to disaster, for it placed the nation at the mercy of a president's ambitions and passions, including perhaps, a consuming interest in his historical reputation. Madison's emphasis on the fact that "among passions of men, dreams of military glory represented a crowning achievement," was punctuated by Hamilton's own dreams of fame and legacy.

Hamilton's contemporaries observed that he had aggressively sought a full-throated war with France in 1798, rather than the limited military activities that characterized the "Quasi-War." Hamilton, it seems, had hoped to engineer the creation of an army of 50,000 men, which he hoped to lead as its commander in chief. Hamilton, it has been observed, "was undoubtedly motivated by his ambition and quest for military fame."[47] But peace was "pernicious," John Adams wrote, to Hamilton's "views of ambition and domination. It extinguished his hopes of being at the head of a victorious army of fifty thousand men, without which, he used to say, he had no idea of having a head upon his shoulders for four years longer."[48]

The Founders' assumption that personal and political interests often drove executive war making raises for us the question of the currency of that premise across the decades. Did American presidents, other leaders and writers view—and fear—executive war-making for similar reasons? If so, should the lessons of history resonate in our time, when the citizenry is confronted with the question of whether the president requires additional power when confronted with the challenges posed by terrorism?

Abraham Lincoln believed that President James J. Polk's instigation of the Mexican-American War derived from his quest for "military glory—that attractive rainbow, that rises in showers of blood—that serpent's eye

---

[46] *Writings of James Madison*, 6:108–109.

[47] Editorial Note, Hamilton Papers, 22:5; quoted in William Michael Treanor, "Fame, the Founding and the Power to Declare War," *Cornell Law Review* 82 (1997), 695, 751.

[48] *The Works of John Adams*, ed. Charles Francis Adams 9 (Free Port, NY, 1969), 309–310.

that charms to destroy."[49] President Nixon thought that war was the surest path to lasting fame. Nixon, an ardent admirer of Winston Churchill, said that by virtue of "his brilliant leadership in WWII," the English Prime Minister had become "a mythical hero who belongs to legend as much as reality, the largest human being of our time."[50] Admiral William Crowe, Chairman of the Joint Chiefs of Staff, observed that President George H. W. Bush's interest in his historical reputation was a motivating factor behind the Gulf War. Admiral Crowe stated: "To be a great president you have to have a war. All great presidents have had their wars."[51]

While it may strike us as counterintuitive, the absence of war, to some presidents, represents a missed opportunity for greatness. Theodore Roosevelt, according to Alan Brinkley, complained frequently that he had been deprived of serving as a wartime president and that Woodrow Wilson had had the real opportunity for greatness. "A man has to take advantage of his opportunities, he observed in 1910, after leaving office, "but the opportunities have to come. If there is not the war, you don't get the great general; if there is not the great occasion, you don't get the great statesman; if Lincoln had lived in times of peace, no one would know his name now."[52]

The prospect that a president might resort to the use of military force as a means of promoting his political standing was, of course, contemplated by the Framers. And they were, as we have seen, acutely aware of the fact that the deployment of military power might serve the ends of the president, but not necessarily those of the nation. Presidents might engage in the use of force or, perhaps, make a show of force for cynical political motives. After surrendering in 1974 the notorious "Watergate Tapes," as ordered by the Supreme Court in the landmark case of *United States v. Nixon*, President Nixon placed American forces on worldwide nuclear alert. There was widespread concern and speculation about his state of

---

[49] Quoted in David H. Donald, *Lincoln* (New York, NY, 1995), 124. (Donald 1995).

[50] Richard M. Nixon, *In the Arena: A Memoir of Victory, Defeat, and Renewal* (New York, NY, 1990), 27. (Nixon 1990).

[51] Quoted in Bob Woodward, *The Commanders* (New York, NY, 1991), 6. (Woodward 1991).

[52] Quoted in Treanor, "Fame," 764.

mind. The tremendous strain of Watergate on Nixon left Americans to wonder at his motives. Fred Emery has written that there "was no question that the alert was linked to Watergate." It is possible that Nixon's action was intended to convey to the Kremlin that the United States remained strong and vital, despite the domestic crisis. Or, as some have speculated, perhaps it represented a political gesture for domestic political consumption "that Nixon might have engineered the crisis to show that he was both in control and personally irreplaceable in the superpower relationship."[53]

If President Nixon had exploited American foreign policy for purely political purposes, perhaps President Reagan could have appreciated his motives. On October 23, 1983, a suicide bomber in Beirut drove through the barriers that surrounded an American compound where Marines were sleeping. The results were devastating. Some 241 Marines were killed and more than 100 others were injured. President Reagan was under intense pressure to explain why American troops on a peace-keeping mission in Lebanon should remain. Reagan insisted that the United States had vital interests in Lebanon but few Americans agreed. Reagan's advisers feared that the devastation in Lebanon would become a major issue in the forthcoming election. Two days after the murder of Marines in Beirut, President Reagan ordered an invasion of Grenada, where the administration said that the lives of U.S. medical students were at stake. Critics disagreed, and saw the invasion as a diversionary tactic. Perhaps Secretary of State George Schultz recognized the opportunity that an invasion presented, when he urged President Reagan to "strike while the iron is hot."[54] The invasion of the tiny island ended in a rout. The American citizenry expressed its approval and it soon moved beyond the concerns about Lebanon. The incident recalls John Quincy Adams' refrain about the achievements of glory through military victory: "A giant obtain[s] glory by crushing a pigmy."[55]

If the Framers feared executive war making as a means of bringing lasting fame and glory, what about presidential interest in the use of military force to win immediate, temporary public support in the form of

---

[53] Fred Emery, *Watergate* (New York, NY, 1995), 408–409. (Emery 1995).

[54] Walter Isaacson, "Weighing the Proper Role," *Time Magazine* (Nov. 7, 1983), 44.

[55] Annals of Congress, 12th Cong., 2d. sess., January 1813), 561.

a spike in the opinion polls, or as a distraction from another event, or to reshape their image and reputation? As we have seen, various scholars have wondered whether Nixon placed America's troops on nuclear alert to shift the public's attention from Watergate, and whether Reagan invaded Grenada to distract from the tragic loss of Marines in Lebanon. What about pursuit of ratings in the polls? President George H. W. Bush, it will be recalled, had been unfairly labeled as a "wimp," despite the fact that he had been a decorated fighter pilot in World War II. However, a successful military invasion of Panama in 1989 to capture strongman Manuel Noriega went a long way toward strengthening Bush's image, Public opinion polls showed that four out of every five people approved of his action. A Pentagon official said the invasion represented "a test of manhood" and a political "jackpot." The surge in popularity was a harbinger of things to come. In 1991, Bush ordered, with authorization from Congress, a large-scale military operation to force Iraq's Saddam Hussein out of Kuwait. The operation, Desert Storm, was an enormous success. As Alexander DeConde observed, "Bush bathed in the glory of a Caesar."[56] Bush enjoyed a skyrocketing public approval rating of 89 percent, the highest figure ever reported in the history of the Gallup Poll.

President Clinton arrived at the White House with no military experience. The perception, in some quarters, that he was a "draft dodger" during the Vietnam War shadowed him and seemed to compromise his status as commander in chief. In June 1993, President Clinton ordered military strikes against Iraq. The attack marked his first projection of U.S. force as President. Reports from the media indicated that the White House understood the utility of the air strikes as a means of shaping "Clinton's image into that of a strong and decisive leader."[57] In 1995, as the Clinton Administration contemplated the deployment of troops to Bosnia as a means of enforcing the Dayton Accords, aides and advisers signaled their awareness of the potential for a political windfall, particularly in the upcoming reelection campaign. The deployment of troops and the projection of military force were again perceived as an opportunity to enhance Clinton's standing as a leader. An aid observed: "One of the things he has

[56] DeConde, *Presidential Machismo*, 249, 255. (DeConde 2000).
[57] Louis Fisher, *Congressional Abdication on War and Spending* (College Station, TX, 2000), 81. (Fisher 2000).

realized over the last two years is that foreign policy can help your image. It makes him look like a President."[58]

Presidential assertions of military force, including war, may yield long-term reputational gains, or merely fleeting success. President George H. W. Bush's spike in the opinion polls did not last long. After all, he was defeated in the 1992 presidential election by Bill Clinton. Bush's standing as a wartime president faded at election time, although most attribute his defeat to a weak economy. His son, President George W. Bush, enjoyed great public support when he ordered in March of 2003, an invasion of Iraq. His premises for the invasion—Saddam Hussein was in league with al Qaeda in the attack on American on September 11, and Hussein possessed weapons of mass destruction—were acknowledged within a year to be untrue. As the war in Iraq unfolded under the leadership of President Bush, and into the Presidency of Barack Obama, the public became increasingly concerned because of its high cost in blood and treasure.

History has its claims on the minds of American presidents. Forrest McDonald has rightly pointed out: "What presidents do in office, or try to, is powerfully influenced by a unique conception of history. The president lives in a museum of the history of the presidency. When walking along the halls of the White House, the president is constantly reminded that Jefferson walked the same halls as he waited for news of negotiations with Napoleon, that Lincoln walked them when waiting for news of Antietam. When dining, the president never escapes the realization that he is using the same silver that Madison and both Roosevelts used. The president understands that he is a member of a mystical fraternity, representing an unbroken chain of history and mythology, and knows that far into the future presidents will be aware that he was a link in that chain, and cannot avoid wondering what his place will be in their memory and the nation's memory."[59]

The concern among presidents about their place in history, in the "nation's memory," is a function of what the Framers attributed to executive leaders across the centuries—the desire for fame, reputation, glory, even immortality. In recent decades, dating at least since the time of President John F. Kennedy, presidents have regularly met with

---

[58] DeConde, *Presidential Machismo*, 269. (DeConde 2000).

[59] Forrest McDonald, *The American Presidency* (Lawrence: University Press of Kansas, 1994), 466–467. (McDonald 1994).

historians to glean from them a historical perspective on the events of their time, how previous presidents have dealt with great issues and challenges and, of course, the question of presidential greatness. Often, the question posed by a president, as it was by Kennedy—"How do you go down in the history books as a great president?"—has been answered by the president before historians can respond. President Kennedy, according to Arthur Schlesinger, Jr., "observed that war made it easier for a president to achieve greatness."[60]

The lessons that the Framers drew from their historical examination of executive war making—the "laurels to be gathered," including fame, glory and reputation, as Madison explained—have resonated throughout the American experience. Moreover, the temptation to aggrandize the war power, even if not for reasons of personal glory and political gain, but rather in pursuit of the foreign relations and national security vision of a single person, invites errors of judgment that may prove fatal to the nation.

THE CLAIM: THE COMMANDER IN CHIEF MAY INITIATE WAR

Unilateral presidential war making, often grounded in the Commander in Chief clause, has become a commonplace. Since 1950, when President Harry S. Truman invoked the office to justify his decision to wage war against North Korea, virtually every subsequent president, including George W. Bush and Barack Obama, has adduced the Commander in Chief Clause as authority to initiate military hostilities. Justice Robert H. Jackson, in his concurring opinion in The Steel Seizure Case (1952), justly stated that the office has been invoked for the "power to do anything, anywhere, that can be done with an army or navy."[61] Of course, the assertion is indefensible.

Indeed, the assertion by presidents from Truman to Obama that the Commander-in-Chief Clause entails authority to initiate military hostilities, including war, collapses under the weight of historical and constitutional analysis. All invocations of the president's power as commander in chief must begin with Alexander Hamilton's explanation in *Federalist No. 69* that the president's authority would be "much inferior" to that

---

[60] Arthur Schlesinger, Jr., "The Democrat Autocrat," *New York Review of Books* 50 (May 15, 2003), 18–19. (Schlesinger 2003).

[61] Youngstown Sheet and Tube Co. v. Sawyer, 343 U.S. 579, 643 (1952).

of the English King and that "it would amount to nothing more than the supreme command and direction of the military and naval forces, as first General and Admiral of the Confederacy."[62] No "first General" may pretend to exercise the bundle of policy-making powers associated with matters of war and peace.

The Framers' decision to vest in Congress, not the president, the constitutional authority to initiate war precludes on grounds of separation of powers and enumeration of powers, executive aggrandizement of authority to order military hostilities. Once delegates settled the matter of the repository of the war power, there remained the matter of determining the scope of the president's authority as commander in chief.

It bears reminder that the office of commander in chief, introduced by the English in 1639 in the First Bishops War, was not conceived as a source of war-making authority. The ranking military official in any theater of battle carried the title of commander in chief, but he always was subordinate to a political superior—the ministry, Parliament, or even the king himself. The duty of that officer was to implement the policies and orders set forth by political officials. The title, and its historical usage, was transplanted in America in the eighteenth century when the Continental Congress on June 15, 1775, unanimously appointed George Washington as "General and Commander in Chief, of the Army of the United Colonies." The instructions drafted by legislators kept Washington on a short leash. He was ordered "punctually to observe and follow such orders and directions" that he "receive" from the Congress.

The practice of subordinating the commander in chief to a political superior, whether a king, parliament or congress was thus firmly established for 150 years, and thoroughly familiar to the Framers. In all likelihood, this settled understanding and absence of concerns about the nature of the office account for the fact that that there was no debate on the Commander-in-Chief Clause at the Convention. In his capacity as commander in chief, the president was expected to conduct war "once authorized or begun." Congress, as we have seen, might authorize the initiation of war, through a declaration or joint resolution. In addition, war might begin with an invasion of the United States, in which case the president was expected to "repel invasions."

[62] Alexander Hamilton, *Federalist No. 69*, at 448.

The era of executive war making, rationalized by assertions of the Commander-in-Chief Clause, rests on the premise of a unilateral presidential power to deploy troops. Does the president possess the *constitutional* power to control troops, including the authority to order them into battle? If so, the president could easily usurp the war power from Congress by inviting or provoking attack, as President James K. Polk did by presenting Congress with a fait accompli after deploying troops into a contested land with Mexico. The president possesses no constitutional power to deploy troops to provoke war. Congress enjoys broad constitutional authority to control troops by virtue of its exclusive authority to decide for war, as well as its "authority to make rules for the Government and Regulation of land and naval forces," the power "to provide for the common Defence," and the power to "raise, support and maintain an army and navy," all located in Article I of the Constitution. Manifestly, the president may not usurp powers granted to other branches of government.

Nor can it be said that the creation by Congress of a standing army conferred upon the president a *constitutional* power to deploy troops. The United States military exists only by virtue of acts of Congress. Since 1789, Congress has passed numerous statutes creating, enlarging and reducing the Army, Navy, and Air force as an exercise of its constitutional authority to "raise and support" the military branches that it has created. The expansive congressional power to "provide for the common Defence" empowers Congress to move troops across the globe to meet its objective.[63] Thus, Congress enjoys plenary discretion in its management of troops; it may, for example, decide to place an army in Iraq, but not in South Korea.

One very effective method of preventing the president from engaging the nation in war was the lack of a standing army with which to take the nation to war. When Congress created a standing army, however, it did not grant to the President authority to deploy troops. Congress maintained the absolute discretion to govern the deployment of troops. As such, Congress might authorize the president to move military forces across the globe. In 1940, for example, Congress passed a statute which provided that "draftees" could not be deployed beyond the limits of the Western Hemisphere. In 1971, Congress enacted a statute that prohibited the use of funds to finance

---

[63] For discussion see Adler, "George Bush as Commander in Chief: Toward the Nether World of Constitutionalism," *Presidential Studies Quarterly* 36 (September 2006), 525. (Adler 2006).

"the introduction of ground troops into Cambodia." Of course, historical convention reflects congressional permission for the president to deploy troops. It bears reminder that the very fact of congressional authorization precludes the conclusion that the president has constitutional authority to deploy troops, but when Congress permits presidential deployment, it should be recalled that what Congress grants, Congress may take away.

Absent constitutional power to deploy troops, the president's ability to plunge the nation into war by provocation is limited, at least to the extent that Congress can summon the will to restrain the president.

THE CLAIM: THE VESTING CLAUSE CONFERS PRESIDENTIAL WAR POWER

Article II, section I of the Constitution provides: "The executive power shall be vested in the President of the United States of America." Since Harry Truman, various presidents and commentators have invoked executive power as a source of presidential power to make war. In 1966, for example, the State Department cited the president's role as chief executive to advance Lyndon Johnson's entry into the Vietnam War. Richard Nixon's legal advisers followed suit to justify his adventures in Southeast Asia. The trend of citing the president's authority as "chief executive" continued, principally as a result of the fact that legal advisers for the president tend to embrace, and invoke, the arguments of their predecessors. Legal briefs for presidents across the years have been consistent, though wide of the constitutional mark.

The claim of executive power as a source of presidential power to initiate hostilities was considered—and rejected—by delegates to the Constitutional Convention. On June 1, it will be recalled, Edmund Randolph introduced a plan for a "national executive," which would have "authority to execute the national laws," and enjoy "the executive rights vested in Congress by the confederation." A pause ensued as delegates contemplated the import of Randolph's proposal. Charles Pinckney voiced the concern of several members of the Convention when he stated that he was "for a vigorous executive but was afraid the executive powers of the existing Congress might extend to peace and war which would render the executive a monarchy, of the worst kind, to wit an elective one." John Rutledge echoed his concern, saying "he was for vesting the Executive power in a single person, tho' he was not for giving him the power of war and peace." James Wilson, influential throughout the proceedings, eased his colleagues' fears. He "did not consider the Prerogatives of the British Monarch as a proper guide to defining the Executive powers. Some of these prerogatives were of a legislative nature. Among others that of war and peace." He added: "Making peace and war are generally determined by writers on the Law of Nations to be legislative powers." Executive powers, he declared, "do not include the Rights of War and peace."

Wilson's explanation calmed the delegates' concerns about the scope of executive power. No delegate to the Constitutional Convention and no member of the various state ratifying conventions, ever suggested or even intimated that executive power was a fountainhead of authority to make war. For the Framers, the term "executive power" was limited to executing the laws and making appointments to office. Certainly, there is no evidence in the records of the Convention to support the claim of presidents since Truman that the concept of executive power is a source of war-making authority. In summary, neither the Commander-in-Chief Clause nor the Executive Power Clause was viewed by the Founders as a repository of presidential power to commence war. The settled understanding was clear: Congress was granted the sole and exclusive authority to decide on matters of war and peace. Lacking textual support in the Constitution, debates in Philadelphia and the state ratifying conventions, not to mention Hamilton's explanation in *Federalist No. 69*, advocates of a unilateral executive war power have turned to the concept of executive prerogative to aid their cause.

THE CLAIM: PRESIDENTIAL PREROGATIVE AND WAR MAKING

Champions of unilateral presidential war making have turned to the Lockean prerogative as a source of executive authority to wage war. Drawing on John Locke's defense of the right of an executive to act for the common good, even if it requires acting in the absence of law or in violation of it, defenders have adduced a similar claim for the president.[64]

---

[64] John Locke, *The Second Treatise of Government*, ed. Thomas P. Peardon (New York: Macmillan, 1986 [1690]). For a discussion of prerogative, see Donald L. Robinson, "Presidential Prerogative and the Spirit of American Constitutionalism," in *The Constitution and Conduct of American Foreign Policy*, eds. Adler and George, 114–132 (Adler and George 1996); Adler, "The Framers and Executive Prerogative: A Constitutional and Historical Rebuke," *Presidential Studies Quarterly* 42 (June 2012), 376–390.

There is not a scintilla of evidence that the Framers intended to incorporate the Lockean Prerogative in the Constitution. In fact, the evidence runs in the other direction. Fears of executive power led the Framers to enumerate the president's powers, to "confine and define" them, in Madison's words as a means of providing security to the people. Clearly, an undefined reservoir of discretionary power in the form of Locke's prerogative would have unraveled the carefully crafted design of Article II and repudiated the Framers' stated aim of corralling executive power. The attribution to the president of a power to wage war in the face of an enumerated grant to Congress to authorize war makes hash of the concept of a written Constitution. And, as John Quincy Adams stated, "The war power is strictly constitutional."[65]

THE CLAIM: THE WAR CLAUSE IS OBSOLETE

One of the principal arguments advanced by advocates of unilateral presidential war making, particularly in the age of terrorism, is the assertion that the Constitution's War Clause is anachronistic. The grant to Congress of authority to initiate military hostilities on behalf of the America people was adequate for the needs of the eighteenth century, but it is not suited, so it is claimed, to the demands of the twenty-first century. That was then, this is now. Of course, the charge of obsolescence is nothing new; it was a commonplace during the Cold War period, in the context of rapid technological change in weaponry, presidents, members of Congress, legal advisers and scholars alike, confronted with the threat of the Soviet Union, urged the removal of restraints on executive war making.[66] It was Dean Acheson, Secretary of State under President Harry Truman, who advised Truman against seeking authorization from Congress before deploying troops into Korea. Acheson, a preeminent member of the American Bar Association and formidable figure in the president's cabinet, told Truman that he enjoyed full authority as commander in chief to deploy troops. But Acheson, who had joined the chorus of voices that touted the availability of a presidential emergency power, went another

---

[65] Cong. Debates 12 (1836), 4037–4038.
[66] See, e.g., Myers McDougal and Asher Lans, "Treaties and Congressional-Executive or Presidential Agreements: Interchangeable Instruments of National Policy," *Yale Law Journal* 54 (1945), 181, 612.

step in testimony before Congress on the question of the constitutional repository of authority to invade South Korea. Acheson declared that, "the argument as to who has the power to do this, that, or the other thing, is not exactly what is called for from America at this very critical hour."[67] If an "official" explanation of the obsolescence of the War Clause was needed, it could be found in a memorandum written in 1966 by the Legal Adviser, Leonard Meeker: In "the twentieth century, the world has grown much smaller. An attack on a country far from our shores can impinge directly on the nation's security ... The Constitution leaves to the President the judgment to determine whether the circumstances of a particular armed attack are so urgent and the potential consequence so threatening to the security of the United States that he should act without formally consulting the Congress."[68]

The concept of a world grown small through powerful advances in weapons technology and information, it has been asserted, has undermined both the fact and desirability of congressional preeminence in matters of war and peace. The obvious sociological, technological, and informational advances over the past 200 years have not authorized the president to revise the Constitution under the concept of "changing circumstances." At its core, the argument, whether characterized as "changing circumstances" or "adaptation by usage," represents a euphemism for the assertion that presidential powers may be expanded without resort to the people, and an attempt to circumvent the Constitution's Amendatory Clause. If there is a demonstrable need for the president to exercise the war-power based, perhaps on the argument that in this dangerous world, the need for "speed and dispatch" is undeniable, then advocates of a shift in power from the president to Congress should introduce a constitutional amendment, as provided in Article V of the Constitution.

Given that the American people, after a vigorous national debate, ratified the constitutional provision—the War Clause—that governed war making, grounded on the premise of "consent of the governed," it is incumbent upon those who urge a change to initiate the process for amending the

---

[67] Arthur Schlesinger, Jr., *The Imperial Presidency* (Boston, MA, 1973), 95–96. (Schlesinger 1973).

[68] Officer of the Legal Adviser, U.S. Department of State, "The Legality of the United States Participation in the Defense of Vietnam," *Department of State Bulletin* 54 (1966), 474.

supreme law of the land. The fact, however, is that this issue has never been explained to the people. Nor has the opinion of the citizenry ever been solicited. Would citizens prefer a system in which a single person makes the decision to plunge the nation into war? Or would they prefer to retain a constitutional system that emphasizes collective decision-making? It is an exercise in elitism to suppose that the people do not care about an issue of such fundamental importance, indeed, one that has affected many families in the United States. Of course people care about who sends them to war, under what circumstances, and upon what grounds. The posture of elitism is magnified by those assert that the people cannot understand an issue of surpassing importance. Of course they can; indeed, they discussed in the process of the ratification debates the question of the repository of the war power, and reviewed explanations and justifications. What is occurring at this juncture is nothing less than presidential usurpation of the war power on the proposition that global contraction implies executive expansion. On what constitutional grounds, the American people are entitled to ask, does the president assert the power to "self-confer" the war-making authority. Certainly Alexander Hamilton was opposed to such a concept. He wrote that a "delegated authority cannot alter the constituting act, unless so expressly authorized by the constituting power. An agent cannot new model his commission."[69]

What is at stake in this theory of changing circumstances is nothing less than the rule of law, the very marrow of which consists of presidential subordination to the Constitution. The executive is a creature of the Constitution and has only that power granted to it by the Constitution; it may do what it is authorized to do and must not do what it is forbidden to do. This theory ignores Article V and substitutes amendment by presidential revision for the solemn deliberation of Congress and the citizenry, as required by the amendatory machinery. Hamilton stated in the *Federalist No. 78*: "Until the people have, by some solemn and authoritative act, annulled or changed the established form, it is binding upon themselves collectively, as well as individually; and no presumption, or even knowledge, of their sentiments, can warrant their representative in a departure from it, prior to such an act."[70]

---

[69] Hamilton, *Works of Alexander Hamilton* 6 (1906), 166.
[70] Hamilton, *Federalist No. 78*, 509.

The Constitutional Convention clearly confined the president, in his capacity as commander in chief, to repelling sudden attacks against the United States. The desire for authority to initiate hostilities requires a constitutional amendment. The doctrine of changing circumstances may not be invoked by the president to justify a presidential revisory authority, unless the nation is prepared to embrace the dispensing and suspending powers that were exercised by the English kings as part and parcel of their prerogative powers. But in the case of the United States, the assertion of those powers, which were rejected, indeed, condemned by the Framers of the Constitution as ill-suited to the republicanism, would permit presidential disregard of constitutional provisions. That doctrine would eviscerate popular sovereignty and government by consent of the people; limited government and, of course, constitutionalism, and the rule of law itself.

The argument about changed circumstances, premised on the alleged obsolescence of the War Clause, runs aground when confronted with the fact that the constitutional constraints imposed on the president in foreign affairs and war-making 200 years ago remain vibrant, vital, and compelling. The question then, as now, pits the values of unilateralism against collective decision-making. If anything, presidential practice across two centuries confirms the wisdom of the original design, for the theory of executive unilateralism, as well as its traditional, underlying arguments, was exploded in the tragedy of the Vietnam War. Advocates of a unilateral executive authority to use military force would reduce Congress to the role of spectator and exalt rule by presidential decree. The argument recalls the pervasive sentiment of the Cold War, and a literature of advice that urged blind trust in the executive on the ground that he alone possessed the information, facts and expertise necessary to safeguard U.S. interests. Rarely has a sentiment been so troubling, dangerous and anti-democratic. It led to the Korean War, the Vietnam War, the imperial presidency, the Iran-Contra Affair, the war in Iraq launched by President George W. Bush, and the ill-advised U.S. invasion of Libya under President Obama. It has led, moreover, to the entrenchment of presidential supremacy in foreign affairs, with its attendant military and policy failures, from the Caribbean and South America to Asia and the Middle East. There is nothing, moreover, in the broader historical record to suggest the conduct of foreign relations by executive elites has produced valuable or wholesome results.

The assertion of the need for speed and dispatch in the use of military force, at any juncture in American history, including the age of terror, is

misguided, dangerous and overrated. Objections abound. The premise—
that presidents need to act quickly to confront emergencies generated by
terrorists, is simplistic. The president, as we have seen, possesses the
authority as commander in chief to repel invasions of the United States.
Everyone agrees with the Framers of the Constitution that if America is
attacked, there is the greatest need to defend the nation. But there is a
world of difference between repelling an invasion of the nation and
initiating military hostilities abroad on the argument that America's
national security has been threatened. Maybe, but maybe not. There are
grave risks associated with presidential determinations of the need to
deploy troops and use force abroad.

The compelling force of the Framers' reasoning in denying to the
president unilateral authority to engage in military hostilities is as powerful
today as it was at the time of the framing of the Constitution. Unless the
nation is attacked, any other use of military power involves a variety of
assessments and calculations, not least of which is the potential threat to
America's security. Some critics of the constitutional design for war are apt
to forget that the founders lived in dangerous times as well. Congress
passed in the early years of the republic dozens of statutes authorizing the
president to respond to emergencies that involved Indian tribes, domestic
tribes, the Barbary pirates, domestic rebellions and various other national
security challenges. The constitutional blueprint for war has worked well
in America's history—when it has been followed. It has been rightly noted
that "the threats confronting the United States during the first quarter
century of government under the constitution imperiled the very independence and survival of the nation. The United States Government
fought wars against France and England, the two greatest powers of that
period, to protect its existence, preserve the balance of power, and defend
its commerce. Notably, both conflicts, the Franco-American War [the
Quasi-War of 1798–1800] and the War of 1812, were authorized by
statute."[71]

Congress, in response to presidential requests, authorized both World
Wars. In fact, Congress issued six declarations of war in World War II.
Since then, it is extremely difficult to cite any instance of unilateral

---

[71] David S. Friedman, "Waging War against Checks and Balances—The Claim of
an Unlimited Presidential War Power," *St. John's Law Review* 57 (1983), 213,
228. (Friedman 1983).

presidential use of force in which the United States has been involved that could not have awaited congressional authorization by Congress, in accord with the Constitution. The asserted need for speed and dispatch simply has not materialized in the circumstances into which presidents deployed American troops. In the case of Korea, it is clear that President Truman had sufficient time to address Congress and seek authorization from Congress. The most compelling case for an immediate presidential response to events in which military force was justified was President Gerald Ford's use of U.S. troops in the evacuation of Americans and foreign nationals from Vietnam.

Beyond that recent history, it is similarly difficult to imagine situations in which the president might need to order military strikes without congressional authorization. An attack on an old and venerable ally, such as Great Britain? Barring a bizarre or outrageous act of provocation by England, it seems clear that the United States would come to the aid of its oldest ally, but the president himself would gather executive aides to discuss America's disposition. Consultation with executive branch officials takes time and in all but very rare cases, the president would have time to seek authorization from Congress.

It has been asserted that the possession of nuclear weapons by American adversaries has exposed the obsolescence of the War Clause. The pursuit of nuclear weapons by additional nations and, perhaps terrorist organizations, it is said, places a premium on the ability of the president to act quickly, and lays bare the sluggish nature of Congress. While it is true that nuclear weapons represent an existential threat to the United States, indeed, to all humanity, the argument here fails to distinguish between the legal ramifications of first and second strike decisions. The decision to initiate nuclear war, as opposed to the initiation of war with conventional weapons, raises no constitutional distinctions; in fact, both require congressional authorization. A second strike in reaction to an attack on the United States would constitute a retaliatory strike, an act within the president's authority as commander in chief to repel sudden attacks.

The assertion that the president should be empowered to order a first use of nuclear weapons raises the same constitutional issues that encircle the broader question of unilateral presidential war making, but the scope and horror of nuclear war brings a razor's edge to the issue of the wisdom of vesting the war power in Congress. The decision to commence war, as we have seen, represents the most solemn, awesome decision any government might make. To place in the hands of the president the awesome authority to deploy an existential weapon places in excruciating context the judgment, vision, temperament, and emotional strength of one person. It raises in our time, as it raised in the Framers' time, the conflict between the values of unilateralism and collective decision-making.

The assertion that the wisdom of one is superior to that of many is philosophically flawed, historically indefensible, and fundamentally undemocratic. Since Aristotle, we have known that information alone is not a guarantee of political success; what matters are the values of the system and, ultimately, those of its decision makers. The implicit trust exhibited by Americans in unilateral executive power in matters of war and foreign affairs over the past seventy-five years has exposed the deficiencies of the presidential perception, judgment and vision. American presidents failed to learn from the French that Vietnam was a quagmire, a failure that confirms John Stuart Mills's rhetorical derision of governmental infallibility. There is "nothing more fallible," wrote James Iredell, a member of the first U.S. Supreme Court and a delegate to the North Carolina Ratifying Convention, than "human judgment," a fundamental philosophical insight reflected in the Framers' implementation of the doctrines of separation of powers and checks and balances, and their rejection of presidential unilateralism.[72]

Advocates of unilateral executive war making often ignore the dimensions of presidential flaws and frailties. Presidents may lack the wisdom, temperament, and judgment, as well as the perception, expertise, and emotional intelligence to achieve success in the realm of foreign relations and national security. The demands of the office are likely to induce strain, stress, and fatigue, which may cause exhaustion, misperception and impaired judgment. Theodore Sorenson remarked: "IK saw first-hand, during the long days and nights of the Cuban Missile Crisis, how brutally physical and mental fatigue can numb the good sense as well as the senses of normally articulate men."[73] Stress and strain may distort perception and judgment. The tragic, final days of Woodrow Wilson's presidency is illustrative: isolation, obstinacy, and distorted judgment undermined his ability to pursue his policy goals. Ronald Reagan's gradual mental deterioration may have preceded the Iran-Contra Affair. Whether Richard Nixon's judgment and mental state were affected by prescription drugs

---

[72] Eliott, *Debates*, 4 (1836), 14.

[73] Theodore Sorenson, *Decision-Making in the White House* (New York, Columbia University Press, 1963), 78. (Sorenson 1963).

allegedly taken in response to depression, the fact that concerns about his mental state led Secretary of Defense James Schlesinger to take the extraordinary step of reminding all military units to ignore orders from "the White House" unless they were cleared by him or the Secretary of State illustrates the grave potential of unilateral presidential power in foreign affairs.

THE CLAIM: PRESIDENTIAL INFORMATION JUSTIFIES WAR MAKING

The assertion that the president is better informed about foreign relations than Congress produces no controversy or argument. But the contention that the superior information justifies presidential deployments of troops or use of force abroad so that he may meet his responsibilities to maintain our national security is an exercise in a series of non sequiturs. First, possession of information entails no authority to act on it. The constitutional allocation of foreign affairs powers, as we have seen, establishes Congress as the senior partner with the president in the management and conduct of the nation's international relations, a hierarchical position which surely entitles it to the information held by the executive. The Treaty Power, comprised of the president and Senate, illustrates the constitutional expectation of shared information. Neither department can make a treaty without the other. And the conferral of authority on Congress to make critical decisions on matters of war and peace would be scuttled if the president withheld information from that constitutional agency. There is, moreover, a correlative duty on the part of the president to share information, a duty set forth in the Constitutional assignment to the president of the responsibility to deliver the State of the Union Address. Justice Joseph Story observed, "There is great wisdom, therefore ... in requiring the President to lay before Congress all facts and information which may assist their deliberations."[74] Second, the issue of whether a nation's actions and policies represent a threat to our vital interests is more a matter of values, perception and judgment, and less a matter of brute fact. As a result, presidential pronouncements are question

---

[74] Joseph Story, *Commentaries on the Constitution of the United States*, 3 vols., 5th edition. 2 (Boston: Little, Brown 1833, 1905), 1561. (Story 1833[1905]).

begging. Third, if a president perceives and declares the existence of a threat to American security interests on the other side of the planet, it does not follow that there is a need for immediate military action, which affords the president time to make his case to Congress. Finally, there is in the Constitution no designation of the president as the nation's leader or guardian in foreign affairs or national security. In any circumstances that may suggest the use of military force, action should not precede analysis and evaluation of the information at hand, as well as the risks, desirability and cost of a military response. All of these factors are better weighed by collective, rather than unilateral, decision making.

CONGRESSIONAL DECISION MAKING

The decision of the Constitutional Convention to vest in Congress the authority over matters of war, as well as the lion's share of foreign affairs powers represented a recognition of the fact, as Madison remarked, that among governmental powers the management of foreign relations is most susceptible to abuse. That conclusion led them to place the aggregate of foreign affairs powers in Congress, not because delegates were under the mystical assumption that Congress was infallible but because they believed that collective decision making was more generally reliable than unilateral executive decision making. In matters of war and peace—the most critical of all decisions—it was important to subject the decision to go to war to the cross fire of debate, on the assumption that, for all of its failings, Congress remains the national forum for debate in which a full airing may be given to all perspectives.

If legislative disagreement on the question of whether the United States should initiate or war or enter a foreign conflict, a disposition that con-tributes to the charge that Congress should not possess the war power in the age of terrorism, that contention and the ongoing deliberations, are the price we pay for renouncing autocracy. Yes—Congress may well frustrate presidential efforts to use military force. Yes—Congress may well move more slowly, far more slowly than many Americans expect. One again, presidential perception of circumstances which he believes requires a military response may not be shared by Congress. If, moreover, legislative disagreement on the question of war is so riven with cracks and fissures that it prevents the formation of consensus on the wisdom and desirability of going to war, then the nation should not go to war until we have reached a consensus. Americans have known the high costs of fighting a war that divided the nation. The divisiveness of the Vietnam War exacted a high cost and yielded valuable lessons, not the least of which was the folly of waging a war without support of the citizenry.

Congressional authorization of military force against terrorists is as necessary today as it was in the early nineteenth century when President Thomas Jefferson faced repeated attacks on American shipping by the Barbary pirates. With the exception of repelling sudden invasions of the United States, as seen in the 9/11 outrage, the question of deploying troops, firing missiles, or using other means of military force against terrorists, require the same careful consideration as that applied to any other commencement of military hostilities. As always, the question raises the issue of the relative merits of executive unilateralism against collective decision-making. Terrorist incidents abroad are unlikely to immediately threaten America's national security interests. Accordingly, there is time for the president to seek from Congress direction and authorization for the use of force. At all events, in those rare circumstances in which the president believes that an immediate use of force is required, without the luxury of time to seek congressional authorization, then the president may wish to deploy force and seek retroactive authorization.

CHAPTER 4

Prescriptions for Protecting
the Constitutional Design for War

Abstract The national security challenges in the age of terrorism do not compel constitutional change. On the contrary, what is required is governmental adherence to those provisions that govern war and peace and national security. In *Federalist No. 51*, James Madison observed that the great challenge confronting America in 1787 was obliging the government to obey the Constitution. That remains the great challenge in our time. Presidents must stop aggrandizing the war power, and Congress must reassert its constitutional authority in the area of war, foreign affairs, and national security. The resurgence of Congress, engagement in vigorous discussion and debate, may well depend upon an aroused citizenry—one committed to the virtues and values of American Constitutionalism and the rule of law, one willing to hold government accountable for the performance of its constitutional responsibilities.

Keywords Constitutional design for war · War on terror · Federalist papers · War clause · War power · Executive supremacy · War and peace · Separation of powers · War powers act of 1973 · Vietnam war

The extraordinary concentration of foreign affairs and national security powers in the American Presidency represents a continuing threat to constitutional principles and republican values. The war power—constitutionally vested in Congress—has long since been aggrandized by the executive, and

© The Author(s) 2017
M.A. Genovese, D.G. Adler, *The War Power in an Age of Terrorism*, The Evolving American Presidency,
DOI 10.1057/978-1-137-57931-7_4

there is little on the horizon to suggest a reversal of the tides of usurpation that have roundly ignored the Constitution. The War on Terror, like the Cold War before it, has supplied a convenient justification for unprecedented expansion of executive authority. The theory of executive supremacy and, remarkably, calls for conferring upon the president even more power, has launched what was, for the Framers, an office of "confined and defined" powers on a trajectory toward the realm of unchecked, unfettered power. Congress, seemingly unwilling to defend its constitutional turf from executive encroachment, has been reduced to the role of spectator. It may be that the constitutional principles, in the words of a former Attorney General in the administration of George W. Bush, have become "quaint" in the context of the "War on Terrorism."

Now, this state of affairs is not what the American people signed up for when they ratified the Constitution two centuries ago. And there is no evidence that the Constitution has been amended to displace the will of the people when it comes to their understanding of the constitutional design for matters of war and peace. Thus far, no advocate of unilateral executive war-making authority has provided a theory that purports to defend a presidential revisory power that is authority to change or even discard the constitutional limitations designed to cabin presidential power. Instead, a nation acquiesces in unilateral executive decisions to use military force, in defiance of the War Clause of the Constitution.

Some, including Professor Genovese, have offered thoughtful contributions to the discussion about the relevance of the Constitution to the twenty-first century and its ongoing confrontation with acts of terror. He is rightly cautious in his conclusion that presidential power "may need to be increased," all the while encouraging more executive consultation with Congress on matters involving the use of military force. As we have learned from our experience under the War Powers Act of 1973, there are precious few means to force the president to consult with Congress even when a statute "requires" it. This is where we are as a nation, as a republic, two centuries into our experiment. We face the essential problem that previous republics faced, and failed to solve: the subordination of the executive to the rule of law.

I have argued in this book that the Constitution—the only one that we have—remains adequate to the national security challenges that we face in the twenty-first century. But there remains the problem of "requiring" government to adhere to its provisions. In *Federalist No. 51*, Madison noted that the great challenge confronting America in 1787 was that of persuading the government to obey the Constitution. Manifestly, it is an enduring challenge. The Framers placed their hopes in separation of powers and checks and balances, along with a dependence on the people to scrutinize governmental actions. The design seemed right. The Framers justly expected that officials, including members of Congress, would vigorously defend their constitutional allocation of powers against efforts by others to encroach on their authority. History suggested, as the Founders explained it, that public officials have a large appetite for power and that the checking and balancing scheme that they intended to employ would, in all likelihood, maintain the constitutional design that the people ratified. The Framers understood that executive power is of a voracious nature, but they assumed that members of Congress would be as well. What the Framers could not have contemplated, of course, was the decline of Congress as a co-equal branch of government, particularly in the realm of foreign affairs and national security.

The decline of Congress has created a vacuum of power filled by the president. Congress, riddled by the problems of excessive partisanship and a paucity of institutional pride, has proved no match for the aggressive assertions of power advanced by the executive. Is it reasonable to assume that Congress might regain its institutional pride and prevent further damage to the Constitution and deterioration of the American Republic? If it is uninterested, or incapable, of recovering its constitutional powers and purposes, then there will be little resistance to the unrestrained exercise of presidential power on matters of war and national security, despite the deficiencies inherent in presidential unilateralism.

A congressional reversal will require leadership, and probably the sort of leadership that is inspired by an aroused citizenry. Of the many passionate speeches delivered by Patrick Henry, the great orator of the American Revolution, few rivaled his speech to colleagues at the Virginia Ratifying Convention, one that shook the rafters when he reached his peroration: "Must I give my soul, my lungs to Congress?" Henry brought a razor's edge to the problem: "If you depend on your President's and Senator's patriotism, you are gone."[1]

In the American Republic, there is no substitute for a vigilant citizenry. "The only real security of liberty," James Iredell stated, "is the jealousy and circumspection of the people themselves. Let them be watchful over

---

[1] Elliot, *Debates,* 3:148–149.

their rulers."[2] In the Virginia State Ratifying Convention, Edmund Randolph echoed the admonitions of his colleague, Patrick Henry and his neighbor in North Carolina, James Iredell: "I hope that my country-men will keep guard against every arrogation of power."[3] The exhortations were pervasive in America at the founding. One wonders what has happened to those sentiments in our time.

CONCLUSIONS

There is, from my viewpoint, no need to further augment presidential power in foreign affairs and national security. In fact, it is not clear that he lacks any power, whether constitutionally conferred or unconstitutionally aggrandized. On the contrary, America's national security interests would be better served by vigorous discussion and debate in Congress on the crucial issues involving the use of military force and renewed assertions of its constitutional powers and responsibilities. But how to achieve this desirable state of affairs? There is no reason to believe that the presidency, home to overgrown powers after decades of usurpation, would return those powers or seek to inspire Congress to rise to its constitutional expectations. Presidents seek power, as we have seen, to meet public expectations. Presidents, like those who seek the office, have little political incentive to decline power. And it is difficult to see members of Congress, tucked safely into their cocoons of comfort and security, created by financial advantages over electoral challengers and gerrymandering, doing much of anything to challenge presidential domination of American foreign policy. Simply put, members have little political incentive to challenge presidential aggrandizement, despite the fact that they have broad constitutional duties to perform in the areas of war and peace and national security.

How to oblige government to obey the Constitution, James Madison asked in No. 51 of the *Federalist Papers*. If presidential humility and congressional resurgence are not forthcoming remedies in our time then, I submit, there is a compelling need for the American citizenry to assert its demands for governmental adherence to the Constitution, including

[2] Elliot, *Debates*, 4:130.
[3] Elliot, *Debates*, 3:207.

loyalty to those provisions that govern the nation's foreign relations. This is a tall order, to be sure. Americans have grown accustomed to executive domination in the field of national security, and far too many, unfortunately, may not see or appreciate the importance of constitutional government and the rule of law. There is a demonstrable need for Americans to acquire an appreciation for the virtues and values of American Constitutionalism, limited government, protection of civil rights and liberties, and the rule of law. Understanding may be drawn from examples of autocrats, authoritarian regimes and examples of unilateral executive acts that have gone terribly wrong. The high price that the United States paid for executive representations and decisions made in the context of the Vietnam War and the invasion of Iraq may be instructive and illuminating. For others, perhaps it will help if they are reminded of the Ghosts of 1776, those leaders who inspired a nation to rally to a cause: denunciation of an imperious executive, oppression, violations of liberties, and disregard of constitutional limitations and the assertion of arbitrary power. America does not need a revolution; it requires a resurgence of republican principles. As the historian Charles McIlwain wrote, "The two fundamental correlative elements of constitutionalism for which all lovers of liberty must yet fight are the legal limits to arbitrary power and a complete responsibility of government to the governed."[4] Who will answer the trumpet call?

---

[4] Charles McIlwain, *Constitutionalism: Ancient and Modern* (Ithaca, Cornell: rev. ed. 1947), 146. (McIlwain 1947).

SELECT BIBLIOGRAPHY

Acheson, Dean. *Present at the Creation: My Years in the State Department.* New York: W. W. Norton, 1969.

Adams, John. *The Works of John Adams.* ed. Charles Francis Adams. Boston: Little Brown, 1856.

Adler, David Gray. "The Constitution and Presidential War Making: The Enduring Debate." *Political Science Quarterly* 103 (1988): 1–36.

Adler, David Gray. "Presidential Greatness as an Attribute of War Making." *Presidential Studies Quarterly* 33 (2003a): 466–483.

Adler, David Gray. "Constitution, Foreign Affairs and Presidential War Making: A Response to Professor Powell." *Georgia State University Law Review* 19 (2003b): 947–1019.

Adler, David Gray. "George Bush as Commander in Chief: Toward the Nether World of Constitutionalism." *Presidential Studies Quarterly* 36 (2006): 525–540.

Adler, David Gray. "George Bush and the Abuse of History: The Constitution and Presidential Power in Foreign Affairs." *UCLA Journal of International Law and Foreign Affairs* 12 (2007): 75–144.

Adler, David Gray. "Jerusalem Passport Case: Judicial Error and the Expansion of the President's Recognition Power." *Presidential Studies Quarterly* 44 (2014): 537–554.

Adler, David Gray., and Larry N. George, eds. *The Constitution and the Conduct of American Foreign Policy.* Lawrence: Kansas, 1996.

Bailyn, Bernard. *The Ideological Origins of the American Revolution.* Cambridge: Harvard University Press, 1967.

© The Author(s) 2017
M.A. Genovese, D.G. Adler, *The War Power in an Age of Terrorism,* The Evolving American Presidency,
DOI 10.1057/978-1-137-57931-7

Bickel, Alexander. "The Original Understanding and the Segregation Decision." *Harvard Law Review* 69 (1955): 1–65.

Blackstone, Sir William. *Commentaries on the Laws of England.* 3 vols. Oxford: Oxford University Press, 1765–1769.

Cardozo, Benjamin N. *The Nature of the Judicial Process.* New Haven: Yale University Press, 1921.

Charles, McIlwain. *Constitutionalism: Ancient and Modern.* rev. ed. Ithaca: Cornell University Press, 1947.

Cronin, Thomas E. *Inventing the American Presidency.* Lawrence: University Press of Kansas, 1989.

DeConde, Alexander. *Presidential Machismo.* Boston: Northeastern University Press, 2000.

DeWeed, Harvey A. *President Wilson Fights His War.* New York: Macmillan, 1968.

Donald, David H. *Lincoln.* New York: Simon and Schuster, 1995.

Eliott, Jonathan, ed. *The Debates on the Several State Conventions on the Adoption of the Federal Constitution.* Philadelphia: J. P. Lipincott, 1861. Reprint; 5 vols. New York: Burt Franklin, 1974.

Emery, Fred. *Watergate.* New York: Crown Publisher, 1995.

Farrand, Max. *The Records of the Federal Convention of 1787.* 4 vols. New Haven: Yale University Press, 1966.

Fisher, Louis. *Congressional Abdication on War and Spending.* College Station: Texas A & M University Press, 2000.

Fisher, Louis. *Presidential War Power.* 3rd ed., revised. Lawrence: University Press of Kansas, 2013.

Fisher, Louis. and David Gray Adler. "The War Powers Resolution: Time to Say Goodbye." *Political Science Quarterly* 113 (1998): 1–20.

Friedman, David S. "Waging War Against Checks and Balances—The Claim of an Unlimited Presidential War Power." *St John's University Law Review* 57 (1983): 213–273.

Gunther, Gerald. *John Marshall's Defense of McCulloch v. Maryland.* Palo Alto: Stanford University Press, 1969.

Irons, Peter. *War Power.* New York: Metropolitan Books, 2005.

Keynes, Edward. *Undeclared War: Twilight Zone of Constitutional Power.* University Park: Pennsylvania University Press, 1982.

Madison, James. *The Writings of James Madison,* 9 vols, ed. Gaillard Hunt. New York: G. P. Putnam, 1900–1910.

McDonald, Forrest. *The American Presidency.* Lawrence: University Press of Kansas, 1994.

Nixon, Richard M. *In the Arena: A Memoir of Victory, Defeat, Renewal.* New York: Simon and Schuster, 1990.

Powell, Jefferson H. *The President's Authority Over Foreign Affairs: An Essay in Constitutional Interpretation*. Durham: Carolina Academic Press, 2002.

Schlesinger, Arthur M. Jr. *The Imperial Presidency*. Boston: Houghton Miflin, 1973.

Schlesinger, Arthur M. Jr. "The Democrat Autocrat." *New York Review of Books* 50 (2003): 18–19.

Sorenson, Theodore. *Decision-Making in the White House*. New York: Columbia University Press, 1963.

Story, Joseph. *Commentaries on the Constitution of the United States*. 3 vols., 5th ed. Boston: Little Brown, 1833[1905].

Woodward, Bob. *The Commanders*. New York: Simon and Schuster, 1991.

Wormuth, Francis D. and Edwin B. Firmage. *To Chain the Dog of War: The War Power of Congress in History and Law*. Dallas: Southern Methodist University Press, 1986.

Yoo, John. "Judicial Review and the War on Terrorism." *George Washington Law Review* 72 (2003): 427–451.

Zeisberg, Mariah. *War Powers*. Princeton: Princeton University Press, 2010.

INDEX

© The Author(s) 2017
M.A. Genovese, D.G. Adler, *The War Power in an Age of Terrorism*, The Evolving American Presidency, DOI 10.1057/978-1-137-57931-7